Praise for *AMA Guide to the Globe*

This is a must-read for anyone doing international marketing research. It is a concise easy-to-read guide.

Martin Block
Medill IMC, Northwestern University
Author, *Business-to-Business Marketing Research*

Holly B. Edmunds' *The AMA Guide to the Globe, Managing the International Marketing Research Process*, is an astoundingly comprehensive guide that starts out with a Q&A section designed to help you decide whether or not you should or should not enter the international market in the first place, followed by exhaustive case studies, research tips, how-to's on proposal preparation, samples of proposals, even software suggestions and up-to-date Web sites to assist in your research. As a international cultural anthropologist, I found that the most fascinating sections are those that cover issues of international ethics, cultural differences, and ideas for crossing language barriers. This is not just a bottom-line guide, but one that helps you understand that, in order to be successful in both economic as well as human terms when venturing beyond national borders, it is essential to be aware of intercultural differences, which can make or break your project.

Dr. Lynne Guitar
Resident Director, Council on International
**   Educational Exchange**
Santiago, Dominican Republic

With research expenses on the rise and business gate-keepers getting tighter by the day, *The AMA Guide to the Globe: Managing the International Marketing Research Process* is an invaluable resource to help navigate through the challenging world of survey research. Research becomes quite complex as you increase the number of countries being addressed, and cells of data to analyze. This book helps put the best course of action into place and trouble shoot when things aren't going exactly as planned.

Lynn Connors LaFiandra, Ph.D.
Director, US Survey Research
Accenture

Just what you need to know. No academic blather. Takes the fear factor away, and provides an approach that makes projects manageable. A good primer for all types of marketing research. Every agency should keep at least one copy, and every new project manager should read it.

Alan Weber
President, Marketing Analytics Group
Adjunct Professor, University of Kansas
Author, *Data-Driven Business Models*

The AMA Guide to the Globe

Managing the International Marketing Research Process

The AMA Guide
to the Globe

Managing the International Marketing Research Process

Holly B. Edmunds

THOMSON

Australia · Brazil · Canada · Mexico · Singapore · Spain · United Kingdom · United States

THOMSON

The AMA Guide to the Globe
Managing the International Marketing Research Process
Holly B. Edmunds

Library of Congress Cataloging in Publication Number is available. See page 315 for details.

For more information about our products, contact us at:

Thomson Learning Academic
Resource Center
1-800-423-0563

Thomson Higher Education
5191 Natorp Boulevard
Mason, Ohio 45040
USA

For Grace
and with thanks and love to
David, James & Rebecca.

Contents

Contents

Contents

Contents

Contents

List of Exhibits and Examples

Introduction

This book is designed to help research buyers make sound decisions regarding the need for and how to conduct international research. The research buyer is not necessarily within a company. A research buyer could also be a vendor—a company that supplies research services to another organization. In either situation, research buyers benefit from guidance on how initiate and carry out research projects that cross national boundaries—or cross cultures within a country.

As one of these research buyers, do you need to expand your currently planned research project to other countries? Or are you a research company project executive who needs to outsource the international portions of a client's study? Some examples of the types of questions that could be answered through international research include:

- For a specific advertising campaign that is prepared to run in the domestic marketplace, is there a need to test the messaging or visuals for any or all of the many European markets?

- How does the youth market vary from country to country in terms of their perceived need for your upcoming new product?

- Will the product features on your prototypes be received equally by American and Asian consumers?

- How do purchase decision processes vary in corporations located in different global markets?

- Will your domestic product packaging be acceptable in other markets?

- How can packaging be used to its best advantage in different countries?

- What about the various segments in your customer base? How do you identify segments within your international customer bases and how will these segments compare to the segments you have already identified in your domestic marketplace?

The decision to conduct research outside of your home country is not a simple one. International research involves weighing considerations of company goals, budget, and timing against cultural preferences and potential returns on your research investment. In addition, there are often multiple decision-makers involved in the approval process to conduct international research—another testament to the importance of "getting it right."

Through a step-by-step discussion of the basic issues and tasks involved in the global research process, this book will help you initiate an international research project, manage the process from the questionnaire development through the project completion of the project and ensure that the results of your project are presented internally. It will help you make research decisions that are educated, well-informed and, above all, in the best interests of your company. Note that this book is not intended to be a technical course in research methodologies; rather, it is designed to be a marketer's guide to managing the overall global research process. Now prepare yourself to think "outside of the box," because international studies can, and frequently do, involve some unusual twists!

1

When to Knock on Foreign Doors

Domestic versus Global Research—
Do You Need It at All?

In prosperous times, companies are more likely to conduct their research in as many markets as they believe are applicable to their product or service. In one of my "past lives" in the technology sector, my research counterparts and I encouraged a global scope to our research projects whenever possible; because our products were global. It did not seem sensible to limit our research to only a domestic study. Indeed, it was not unusual to conduct, for example, a series of several focus groups in three different markets in the United States, three countries in Western Europe and one or more Asian markets.

In somewhat leaner economic times, however, there is a concerted effort to approach the research process from a "how little can we get away with?" perspective. Ironically, this is the preferred philosophy in that you are forced to weigh the potential value of the proposed research against the costs that will be incurred in conducting the study. If, for example, you represent an American company with a sales base located in the domestic marketplace, it may not be worthwhile to conduct research in your much smaller Latin American market if you are not willing to make some changes to a product, program or marketing plan based on the research results. If you are willing to consider making changes, conduct that additional research. On the other hand, if you are introducing a new product or service to *all* of your markets, at home and abroad, you must conduct research in order to consider fully the cultural differences regarding its acceptance.

Be forewarned, however: If you are going to do it, do it right! Global research projects have their own particular costs, and when they are conducted by an inexperienced firm or using the wrong methodology, the resulting data can lead to the wrong decisions, resulting in even greater expense.

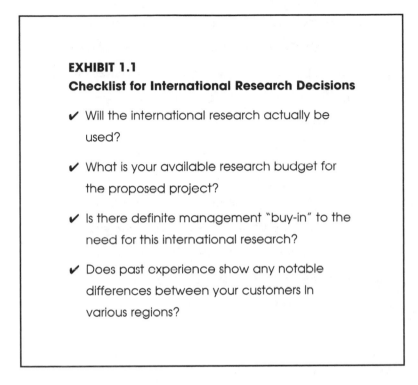

EXHIBIT 1.1
Checklist for International Research Decisions

✔ Will the international research actually be used?

✔ What is your available research budget for the proposed project?

✔ Is there definite management "buy-in" to the need for this international research?

✔ Does past experience show any notable differences between your customers In various regions?

The checklist in Exhibit 1.1 will help you assess the value of conducting a market research project in one or more foreign countries.

Useful and Usable

Will the results of the research be actually used to decide which country(ies) you may want to enter? Which country(ies) do you want to include in the study? If your organization is not likely to apply recommendations resulting from the proposed research study in certain

21

countries, reconsider the logic of conducting the project in those countries. While the research should provide insights, without a willingness to address issues that arise, the research will not be useful enough to warrant the costs incurred in the process.

You should seriously consider where you will be able to use information from the research to help you make the best use of your available research budget. As a very elementary example, if you are certain that you will have a marketing budget for only the US market and one other *English-speaking* market, research in Italy or China would not be likely to prove immediately useful.

Budget

International research studies can be more costly than the typical domestic research study. Costs are increased by factors such as translations (possibly into multiple languages) of questionnaires, packaging, promotions, discussion guides and other materials, as well as the need for project-related travel and potentially increased project management costs. Are you certain that your budget will allow you to conduct the required research both domestically and internationally? If not, you need to determine where the budget will be most effective.

Among your alternatives:

- You can conduct the study in your home country only.

- You can conduct it internationally only.

- You can reduce the number of countries.

- You can (maybe!) reduce the number of issues to be researched.

- You can reduce the sample sizes per country or region, keeping in mind your data must be statistically significant if they are to be reliable for making decisions and meeting your objectives.

Furthermore, if the study is vital to making strategic management decisions, the project should have funds sufficient to ensure that the study will provide the best (not necessarily the most) detail in all pertinent markets. It is better to allocate extra budget now than to pay later to correct decisions made using less than adequate data.

Management Commitment

Is there definite senior management "buy-in" to the need for this international research? Does your organization's management support your research initiative?

Without support of your management and others affected by the research topic, the research results are not likely to be put to good use. If the ultimate decision-makers do not see research as an integral part of the marketing process, this issue should be addressed prior to incurring the expenses inherent in conducting international research. Likewise, if they do not understand the international research process, they will not be likely to use the results to their fullest potential.

In addition, if the company already has a presence in a country to be researched, it is important to bring that management and possibly others to the table for planning the research whenever applicable and feasible. If they are included in the planning process, they are more likely to support decisions made in their regions as a result of the research. Furthermore, they can be very helpful in terms of assisting with the implementation of the research with the identification of accurate lists or reliable sample sources, gaining cooperation of channel partners for project-related tasks, and so forth.

The Value of Experience

Does past experience show any notable differences between your customers in various regions? Has your organization ever conducted research outside your domestic market? If so, some of the findings of that other primary and/or secondary research may apply to your current project. They may provide relevant insights into the mindset of businesses or consumers in certain of your current and/or potential foreign marketplaces. Are there certain issues included in those studies that you see having the potential to help you determine if your current research would be a crucial component to decision-making?

For instance, American and British research audiences frequently respond with very similar reactions to certain topics. Information Technology (IT) managers in London corporations have needs very similar to their management equivalents in New York or Chicago. However, they may also have differences, such as smaller office spaces, resulting in the need for more compact equipment. While it may not be necessary to research the same issue a second time for the same client, the differences should still be noted in the report because those evaluating the new research may not be aware of the "old" research, or previous readers may need to be reminded.

If, for cost reasons, research can be conducted in only one market, choose the one which has the most potential for growth in a new direction, or has recorded the most complaints, for example.

A word of caution is definitely needed here. Do not make the mistake of assuming, for instance, that the cultural preferences and buying habits of all Hispanics in the United States are the same as or are indicative of responses of Latin Americans elsewhere, not even in their own home nations. There are invariably going to be differences among these respondents, given their day-to-day environments, the political environments and economies in which they live, and the media to which they are regularly exposed.

Likewise, one cannot assume that other segments of populations (e.g., Chinese-Americans in San Francisco or

Indians in the United Kingdom) will respond in the same way as Chinese nationals or Indians residing in New Delhi or even Mumbai (Bombay). Do not expect to use such assumptions as an inexpensive substitute for true research.

Making the Jump: Going Global

As noted earlier, the purpose of this book is not to teach specific research methodologies. It is assumed that you have a basic understanding of market research and its conduct in the domestic market, regardless of whether that market is in the United States or in France. The concern we address here is how to take your research knowledge and apply it to a project in one or more international markets.

I assume that at this point you have made the decision that indeed your marketing department needs to conduct an international research study. To make the process explanations flow more clearly over the course of the book, select either an existing issue your company has or choose one from the following list of generic situations.

Potential Research Situations

The following represent potential research situations:

- Testing a series of advertisements for a product which is available in the domestic market and which you plan to introduce to several international markets.

- Testing product features on a prototype hand-held personal computing device in several markets, including the domestic market.
- Evaluating customers' attitudes regarding customer response programs in several countries.
- Evaluating your brand recognition in a number of international regions.

Some more specific examples of business issues leading to global research and its eventual results are presented in the following four case study summaries.

Case Study Summary 1.1

A major computer manufacturer needed to identify the best configuration of features for a new product as well as how to position this new product within its existing product portfolio.

The research ultimately conducted involved focus groups in North America, Europe and Asia-Pacific. The project also included a quantitative trade-off exercise by focus group participants prior to each of the group discussions.

The results of the study identified potential customer segments for the new product as well as the key product features/specifications that would most appeal to each of those segments. In addition, it provided solid recommendations for marketing of the new product and additional recommendations for future product development considerations.

Case Study Summary 1.2

A manufacturer of consumer products needed to measure customer satisfaction on a global basis. Its key objective for the proposed research was to provide its managers in each local office worldwide with tools for improving retention of key accounts.

The market research supplier recommended and conducted face-to-face or telephone interviews, depending on the regions where the study was conducted, with key customer account representatives. Interviews were also conducted with the manufacturer's primary competitors' customers in each region.

The resulting research data was able to identify key service strengths versus major weaknesses. Likewise, the research results identified accounts that should be classified as "at risk." The report provided recommendations on how the client could best address poor performance issues and leverage managers' strengths in order to maintain and grow their customer accounts.

Case Study Summary 1.3

A cellular telephone hardware manufacturer wanted to test the usability of its Web site among its various target customer sectors.

The research design consisted of multinational focus groups consisting of network operators, business users, and other pre-identified customer categories.

The expansive qualitative study resulted in recommended changes to the Web site that addressed specific concerns as well as leveraging information to correct brand perceptions on the Web site.

Case Study Summary 1.4

A global online consumer retailer required an evaluation to identify customers' as well as potential customers' requirements for electronic customer services. A key concern was how to make this aspect of its Web site attractive to a variety of regions and easily understood in a range of languages.

The client's selected research vendor designed and coordinated a Web survey among the retailer's newsletter subscribers as well as among noncustomers within appropriate demographics within each region.

The recommendations of the respondents resulted in design revisions and usability improvements, making the client's electronic customer service solution "state-of-the-art" while still being user-friendly.

Internal Considerations

Once you have determined that you do require international research and have identified the general "reasons
why" you need to conduct the study, it is then necessary
to determine how to go about setting up the project. First,
there are the internal considerations reflected in Exhibit
1.2.

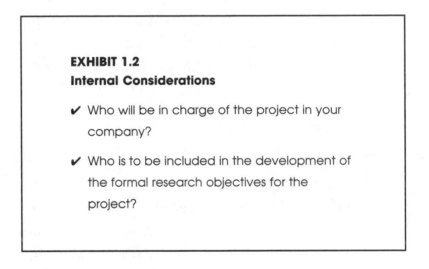

EXHIBIT 1.2
Internal Considerations

✔ Who will be in charge of the project in your
company?

✔ Who is to be included in the development of
the formal research objectives for the
project?

Project Management

Who will be in charge of the project? In many companies,
internal researchers or research departments can handle
project management. In other situations, you and/or a
team of product managers and/or marketing staff may run
the project. In any case, it is important to establish an internal line of authority from the start to make it easier

and more efficient to finalize questionnaires and other project-related materials. You will also need to authorize someone to deal with any outside research suppliers.

This holds true as well if you are a vendor research company using subcontractors to assist in international projects. You are the client to these subcontractors and need to establish these processes and roles with your subcontractors from the start.

Development of Objectives

Who is to be included in the development of the formal research objectives for the project?

If you are the company's internal research liaison or designated team leader, the responsibility of getting the actual research project done will fall directly on you. Typically, however, the research objectives have originated elsewhere in the company. Depending on the issues at hand, one or more groups within the company may have a vested interest in the research results and therefore also should play a role in developing the objectives for the study. These can include, but are not limited to, marketing managers, product managers, design engineers, customer relations managers, supply chain managers, advertising agency account teams and so on.

Your role will most likely involve sorting through all of the available inputs to identify the key objectives versus those that are secondary to the objectives and those that may not at all fit the research to be conducted. Basically, you will be required to separate the "need to know" items from the "nice to know" and "not to know now" items. Remember that a single research study may not be able to answer everything for everyone!

Drafting the RFP

The next question is, Who will draft the Request for Proposal (RFP)? It is strongly recommended that the person who will be the primary internal project manager of a given research project at your company be the person responsible for writing the Request for Proposal (RFP). Regardless of who is actually writing the RFP, you should always ensure that at least one other project team member reviews the draft document to check for any possible errors. These errors can occur either in the form of simple typographical errors or, worse, in the technical specifications for the project, including your objectives. Remember that the RFP is your best means of reducing misunderstandings with any research suppliers from the start.

Chapter 1 Take-Aways

☑ Decide if research is needed:

- Identify the purpose of the proposed research.

- Determine if the proposed international research will be used.

- Identify the available project budget.

- Confirm management "buy-in" regarding the research.

- Select regions/countries that will provide inputs crucial to your decision.

☑ Set the research in motion internally:

- Identify the person who will be in charge of the project at your company.

- Determine who will help develop the research objectives.

- Assign someone to draft the Request for Proposal.

r

2

Getting the Process Started

Once the responsibilities for these tasks have been identified and assigned, the Request for Proposal (RFP) process can begin. The checklist in Exhibit 2.1 provides general guidelines as to what details should be included in your RFP.

Obviously, the more details about your primary objectives and your anticipated research requirements that you are able to provide, the better the responding research

EXHIBIT 2.1
A Checklist for Preparing the Request for Proposal

✔ A brief background of the study

✔ Key research objectives

✔ "Sub" objectives—"like to know" versus "need to know" information

✔ Timing for proposal delivery and for research results

✔ Methodology being considered

✔ Countries to be targeted

✔ Specifications for target respondents

✔ Suggestions for sources of samples

✔ What you expect the supplier to provide

✔ The role you expect to play in the research process

✔ Required proposal format

✔ Your available budget

✔ Your contact information

✔ Proposal submission process

suppliers will be able to properly address your specific research needs.

Background

What prompted you to conduct the research in the first place? Your answer should be a short but clear summary of the problems or issues that led to your RFP. Explain why your company needs answers to these questions rather than what precise answers your team expects to gain from the study. This should be a concise description of the problem or concern itself.

Key Objectives

What decisions will be made based on the results of the research? These are the expected solutions to the problems or issues that prompted this research study. These points should be very clearly defined and specific in terms of what you need to find out. This is a list of specifically what you must learn in order for the research to be successful. (This does not, of course, suggest that you will necessarily get the answers you prefer or expect, but rather that your questions will be answered correctly based on your targeted respondents.)

Typically there will be two or three key objectives: "need to know" items that your research must provide answers to and potential solutions for. You should avoid including too many main objectives because it will either make your costs and/or your data unmanageable!

"Sub" Objectives

Don't try to force one research study to accomplish too many things. Invariably, managers will approach you with requests to incorporate "just a couple of quick questions" concerning their own key "issues du jour" into your research study. If their subject matter is closely related to the research topics you will be investigating, it may actually be more cost-effective for the company to gain some initial insights via your study.

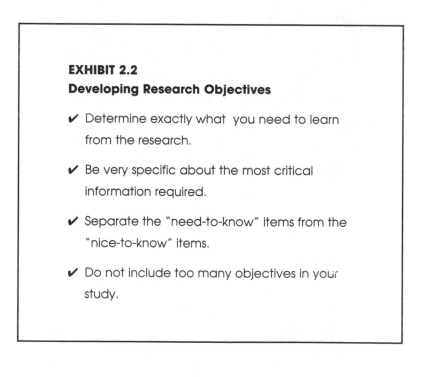

EXHIBIT 2.2
Developing Research Objectives

✔ Determine exactly what you need to learn from the research.

✔ Be very specific about the most critical information required.

✔ Separate the "need-to-know" items from the "nice-to-know" items.

✔ Do not include too many objectives in your study.

When, however, the requested topic is outside of the anticipated scope of your research, it will only add unnecessarily to the length of your questionnaire or discussion guide without contributing to your primary objectives. This is when you should speak up and avoid including these extra questions in your project.

Timing

Be realistic when providing your schedule expectations to potential research suppliers. Allow adequate time for the vendors to develop their proposals. Remember that they need to prepare detailed estimates, which for international projects will typically take more time than doing so for your familiar domestic market. From a vendor's perspective, nothing can cause nightmares quite like being given only a one- or two-day turnaround time to meet your deadline.

Such requests are not realistic and can end up costing you in the long run because you did not allow enough time to consider all the necessary details that should normally be addressed at the outset. It is worth the additional time in the proposal phase to ensure that all possible research options are considered.

Likewise, ask each of the suppliers who are bidding on your study to provide a detailed timeline that gives you a realistic schedule regarding sampling, fieldwork, data processing, analysis and reporting.

Methodology

What do you/your team envision in terms of how the research will be conducted? From past experience with research for your organization, you and other members of your internal team may have some good ideas regarding what methodology will work best on this project. By all means, include your methodology recommendations in the Request for Proposal. If possible, specify why you believe this would work well in this instance.

Remember, however, that you are seeking proposals from research experts. Presumably, they have more experience with international research than you and your team. They may have other better recommendations. Be willing to consider different methodologies included in their proposals and ask them to provide details regarding their recommendations.

While your suggested methodology is not necessarily inappropriate for the situation, your bidding suppliers may provide alternate solutions that will could provide better analytical capabilities, more cost-effective processes or simply be more easily applied in the countries where the research will be conducted.

Target Countries

Give the reasons why you are considering research in the specific market(s). Is your company experiencing the problems or becoming aware of subjects of interest that initially prompted this particular research in certain countries or regions more than in others? The more countries or regions you decide to target with this research, obviously the greater your research expense will be.

It is important to evaluate carefully where you believe the research will prove to be most effective for your specific business needs. A word of caution: Avoid allowing managers who want to accumulate frequent flyer miles to drive the selection of the foreign locations for the research!

Specify Your Target Respondents

Always include as many details as possible that you expect will have an impact on your findings. Describe the people you expect to answer your questions and explain why they are considered to be the key targets.

For consumers these details can include such data as age, income levels, education, gender, marital status, religious affiliation, employment status and/or profession, number of children residing within their households, ethnic background, and so on. For businesses, consider including factors such as their decision-making processes, numbers of years of experience in a given field or within their current organization, educational/professional backgrounds, size of company, annual sales, number of employees on site and/or other criteria.

If you have a solid estimate of the incidence of target respondents in the overall sample universe, provide that information as well, because this will allow vendors to provide more accurate cost estimates. For example, if you want to measure customer satisfaction among users of your product "X," you should attempt to provide those vendors who are bidding on the research with a total count of how many of your customers purchase product "X."

Sample Sources

Identify the level of detail you will be able to provide in your list of suggested sources—i.e., email addresses, contact names, direct telephone numbers, mailing addresses, etc.—and in what formats the list will be available (CD, hard copy, etc.).

In addition to your own company listings, you may actually be able to provide other sample sources for your research study. For example, does your company have a subscription to the Dun & Bradstreet database? If so, consider whether this could be a "fit" in terms of identifying potential research respondents or focus group participants.

Also, be upfront with the suppliers if you are certain that you will not be able to provide the sample and emphasize that provision of appropriate sample lists is expected to be included in their proposals.

What the Supplier Provides

There are two levels to what you might expect a supplier will have to provide. You should be clear about this at the beginning.

First, what do you expect the vendor to provide in terms of deliverables? Be as specific as possible. I strongly suggest that you request that each deliverable and its associated costs to be separately itemized in the vendors' proposals.

Deliverables can be actual documents or completed research tasks and could include, but not be limited to, the following:

- Screeners
- Questionnaires
- Focus group discussion guides
- Web survey programming
- Sample lists
- Focus group recruitment
- Survey fieldwork (interviewing)
- Focus group facility reservations/arrangements
- Data tabulations/analysis
- Executive summary report
- Presentation

Second, you should also indicate any project management roles you may expect your research supplier to cover. These can include a wide variety of expectations, but you will not necessarily see these as separate line items in the vendors' estimated budget.

Some possible issues to note in this category could include:

- Providing regular (daily, weekly, etc.) status reports.
- Validation of a predetermined percentage of completed surveys.
- Coding of open-ended questions.
- Updated briefings of interviewers if significant changes are made to the project and/or the questionnaire.
- Ongoing monitoring to ensure quality of survey responses.

The Client's Role

Just as you have listed all of your expectations of the vendor in terms of the deliverables and tasks, you should also specify your internal team members' anticipated roles in the proposed project. Open communications between the research vendor and the client are key to the success of the project. Both sides should respond quickly and honestly to questions related to the study. Don't be afraid to express any concerns you might have. Be an active participant in your research study.

Following are some possible items to include among your planned responsibilities in this section of the RFP:

- Provision of inputs to screeners, questionnaires and discussion guides.
- Provision of sample(s) as appropriate and available.
- Approval of/formal sign-off on all research project materials.
- Active participation in the project briefing.
- Monitoring of initial interviews/pre-test of the study.
- Attending focus groups/in-depth interviews.
- Participating in debriefings following focus groups/interview sessions.
- Decisions regarding data base banners and cross-tabulations.
- Inputs to and approval of reports.
- Evaluation of/inputs to/participation in the final research presentation.

Required Proposal Format

What do you expect the RFP to look like when you receive it? Do you expect the bidding vendors to provide a brief memo format in lieu of a formal proposal or would you prefer a longer, more detailed document? Detailed research proposals can range in length from 8 to 40+ pages, depending on the scope of your proposed research needs, the specific methodology required and the regions expected to be covered in the project.

While the memo format may seem more attractive in terms of saving you a great deal of time when you evaluate them, by allowing quick comparisons of a few two- or three-page "proposals," it is important to bear in mind that you will lose a great many of the details which could be crucial in evaluating the bids. The majority of important aspects related to how your study will be conducted (i.e., the sampling process, details related to selected and often complicated methodologies, etc.) may be missing from such consolidated versions of proposals.

Request that suppliers include any information that you feel will help you make the best possible vendor selection for your research. Consider asking for the firms' overall credentials as well as biographies of the key vendor project team members, although they should offer them in their proposals.

Budget

There are potential positive and negative effects to providing potential vendors with your estimated budget range. On the downside, you obviously run the risk that vendors will develop a proposal that will use every available dollar. A positive aspect, however, is that having a price range to work within allows vendors to tailor their proposals to avoid "overshooting" your anticipated budget ceiling.

Regardless, you should expect that vendors will attempt to provide you with everything from "soup to nuts" in their proposals. It is up to you to discern what you absolutely require in terms of professional research services and what you can eliminate without losing important data. It is helpful to request that the suppliers provide detailed breakdowns of their cost estimates to assist you in evaluating what you absolutely need and what you will be able to cut without negative effects on your study.

It is, of course, obvious that international research projects will vary in their costs, given the scope, methodology, number of regions and targeted audience. There are, however, some very basic "rules of thumb" to use when developing a budget for your research project.

Focus groups are usually the easiest to generalize in terms of costs. For a single 90-minute to two-hour group with 8 to 10 participants, you can expect to pay between $6,000 and $8,000 US dollars. This should be an all-inclusive price covering everything from the design and recruiting to facility rental and refreshments, moderation, and reporting.

You can expect to pay for translation and interpretation. You can expect to pay more for high level executives compared to general consumers, both in recruiting and in cooperative payment costs.

Furthermore, you will need to consider the travel costs for all necessary attendees from your team.

The location of the markets you are including can also affect your costs. For example, Paris, Tokyo and New York are much more expensive markets to cover, and you should consider if the return will be worthwhile for you in terms of your objectives.

Quantitative research projects are much more difficult to budget for because of respondent incidence and completion rates, questionnaire length, required quota categories and the methodology used.

While it is impossible to give solid guidelines for budgeting quantitative studies, you should expect that the professional fees involved in the project will encompass between 14 percent and 20 percent of the total project cost. It is this portion of the study that you will be better able to negotiate with the vendors, as it is what they have the most control over.

Fieldwork costs are based primarily on the incidence of the target respondents and the length of the questionnaire. You can cut these costs by changing the respondent specifications, the number of total completed interviews required, or the number of questions being asked. If a vendor is subcontracting the fieldwork, it is, however, likely that a mark-up is being added to the fieldwork costs to allow some margin to be earned by your primary vendor. This also may allow you some room for negotiation.

Suppliers' Questions

To whom should the vendors address their questions? It is crucial that you clearly indicate the person who will be responsible for answering questions and providing information pertinent to the supplier. The proposals you receive will only be as good as the information the vendors have to work from, so it is important to have someone available to answer pertinent questions related to your request for proposal.

Typically, vendors will send the proposal directly to the person who sent them the initial RFP. However, if suppliers are to respond to someone else for some reason, you need to provide detailed instructions regarding who should receive the proposal.

Also, if at all possible, you should be certain to identify an alternate contact just in case the primary internal contact person is unavailable when the questions come up.

For any contact person listed, you should provide as much information as possible, such as telephone numbers, email addresses and fax numbers if applicable.

Proposal Submission

What is the fastest, most convenient way for the research vendors to deliver their proposals to you? Typically, email is being used to turn proposals in, as email allows the vendor to complete cost estimates and double-check all of the necessary details until the very last minute. Some, however, prefer to deliver a hard copy, whether via fax or overnight express delivery service or other means.

Be explicit in your instructions as to whom the proposal should be addressed and identify any additional members of your team who should also receive a copy of the proposal. Provide all bidders with all of the necessary contact information for reaching each team member who is involved in the bid decision-making process. Include all applicable email addresses, telephone numbers, fax numbers, mailing addresses, etc.

Late proposals, proposals not sent correctly to the entire distribution list, or proposals that have numerous typographical errors may signal future management problems. If a vendor is not taking adequate pains to avoid such sloppiness during the crucial bidding phase of your research, then what will happen during the actual project?

One London field director provides her project executives with detailed staff training, which includes a basic list of questions to ask potential clients when they call in to request proposals for research fieldwork (see Exhibit 2.3). Because her outline addresses primarily quantitative survey fieldwork, I have taken the liberty of adding a number of italicized items that address other potential research needs as well.

EXHIBIT 2.3
Quote Requests

Type of Interviews

- Telephone, face-to-face, Web

- CATI, pen and paper, taped and transcribed

- Telephone, phone/fax, email, Web/phone, Web-assisted

- Focus group screening/recruitment (traditional groups, dyads, triads, Web)

- Depth interview screening/recruitment

Number of Interviews

- A breakdown, if appropriate, i.e., how many customers/non-customers or how many per country, etc.

- Types of interviews: business-to-business, consumers, non-profits, etc.

Location

- Domestic—which regions?

- International—what countries?

EXHIBIT 2.3 Continued

Type of Company

- Micro businesses

- SMEs (Small to Medium-sized Enterprises)

- Large corporations

- Multinational corporations

- How are they defined? (i.e., # of employees, turnover, etc.)

Business Respondents

- Job title or area of responsibility

- Level (i.e., manager, senior manager, board member, etc.)

- Professional status (i.e., legal, medical, etc.)

Consumer Respondents

- Age

- Gender

- Income level

- Educational background

- Profession

- Other demographics

EXHIBIT 2.3 Continued

Subject

- Brief description of the subject matter

Client Information

- Client's name or, if that is not possible,

- A description of client (i.e., internationally recognized pharmaceutical company)

Disclosures

- Will we be allowed to tell respondents the name of the client and, if so, at what point in the interview (i.e., introduction, mid-way or not until the end)?[1]

- Specify if an NDA (non-disclosure agreement) will be required (for the supplier, interviewers/moderators and/or the participants/respondents)

Quotas/Qualifying Criteria

- Brief description of any eligibility or qualifying criteria and an outline of quotas

Sample Required

- Linked to the above: if client sample will be provided, in what ratio?

EXHIBIT 2.3 Continued

Time Restrictions

- If it is not definitely known, always include a request for estimated time to complete fieldwork

Incentives

- Individual incentives (i.e., gift, prize drawing entry, cash)
- Charity donation
- Summary report
- Other: _____

Deliverables

- Tables
- Data file (what format, whose data map?)
- Charts/graphics
- Report (specify format: Top-line? Summary? Detailed?)
- Presentation (in-person, conference call or videoconference, etc.)

Translation

- Translation required or provided (request back-translation)

Combined, these listed items certainly provide an excellent general guideline to follow when drafting your own RFP in terms of what details you should be prepared to provide to the bidding research suppliers. My colleague's comment regarding this list is that ". . . this is 'ideal world' stuff, and it's often the case that not all of this will be known at the RFP stage. Still a girl can dream, can't she?!"

Obviously, the more information which you are able to provide suppliers with upfront, the better the guarantee of accuracy in both their estimated costs as well as their recommended methodology.

In Example 2.1 are details of an RFP sent by a client to several research suppliers. Note the level of detail that the suppliers are requested to provide in their proposal.

Proposal Evaluations

Criteria used in selecting the vendor will include:

- experience with procuring hard-to-reach, smaller samples
- ability to conduct a blind survey of this audience
- quality of Web survey programming (or conduct quality phone interviews)
- ability to employ flexible, creative and effective methods for data capture when initial sample procurement proves insufficient

Text continues on page 59

Example 2.1
SOFTWARE TRACKING
REQUEST FOR PROPOSAL

Software Marketing Development Company
September, 20—

Software Marketing Development Company (SMD) sells 4 professional database products: Level A, Level B, Level C and Level D. Each of these products can be purchased individually or four products can be purchased in one of two bundled products called Bundle A and Bundle B. In addition, customers can purchase products directly, through resellers or via OEM bundles.

SMD realizes in order for the market to perceive our database line as a professional line, our products need to be respected by and used by database professionals.

Project Objectives

The main objective of this research is to measure and track SMD's performance selling database software to its targeted markets.

Detailed objectives include:
- Measure and track product buying cycle process (awareness, interest, consideration, purchase, and loyalty) for the primary products in the three SMD database software categories.
- Measure and track purchase channels (direct, reseller, bundle) used when procuring database software.

Project Requirements and Deliverables

Methodology
Following is SMD's current thinking on the approach to the research. However, we would welcome any alternative methodologies if they are better at achieving the objectives listed in the previous section.

Example 2.1 Continued

Data collection methodology: Blind Web-based survey
Geographic scope: United States/Canada/United Kingdom/Australia
Language: English only
Sample: Please recommend potential sources
Our preference is that SMD should not be identified as the sponsor of the study to minimize bias regarding unaided awareness and perceptions of our products relative to our competitors' products.

Survey Instruments

SMD will coordinate the survey development, but expects the selected vendor to thoroughly review the survey and make recommendations on improvements before implementing the study.

Project Management

The supplier will prepare a project plan with a detailed schedule for conducting the research. The plan shall include: business objectives, reporting/analysis outline, methodology, resource allocation, and timing. The supplier and SMD will review the plan to ensure the design will answer intended questions. SMD will provide comments to the supplier who will incorporate comments and deliver a final project plan.

The supplier will provide a weekly progress report showing any variance to the schedule or budget from the previous week and identifying reasons for any variance. Project milestones should include:

- Kick-off meeting for the project
- Finalizing objectives and reporting/analysis outline
- Survey design: draft, feedback, finalization
- Programming survey for the Web, review Web survey, finalize
- Pre-test Web survey
- Fielding survey
- Banners, SPSS data file
- Work session report
- Final report

(Continued on next page)

Example 2.1 Continued

Cost Breakdown

SMD would like to see the cost of the project broken down into the following areas, for each geography:

- Sample
- Project management, including weekly updates, survey programming and field management
- Data preparation and development of cross-tabulations
- Reporting

Please itemize your costs so that we can identify areas where adjustments can be made to reduce scope and/or cost.

Schedule

Please provide a schedule for the project based on the kick-off date and other project limitations:

- Kick-off Meeting
- Field Survey
- Top-line Report
- Work Session
- Final report

SMD will analyze responses to select a vendor who best meets the overall requirements. Please state all assumptions made throughout the proposal and for itemized costs.

Ongoing questions during the vendor's proposal preparation will be answered by: Arlene Smith, SMD, asmith@smd.com.

One electronic copy of the bid in PDF format is due no later than September 18th by 5 p.m. EST.

- industry experience (relevant to SMD and database software, in particular)
- timely reporting capabilities (*e.g.,* real time Web reporting of fielding statistics and response frequencies)
- Senior-level, experienced project management team

  Please provide details on how and where you will procure sample, not just for the first wave, but for subsequent waves as well.

  Please provide a description of the project team members along with their relevant experience and credentials. Please provide references for your company and for project team members. We will ask them about their satisfaction with the working relationship and the actionability of the results.

As you develop your RFP, you might want to use the example in Exhibit 2.4.

EXHIBIT 2.4
Building Your RFP

Business Issue/Background:

_____

_____

Key Research Objectives:

1) _____

2) _____

3) _____

Target Audience (demographics/business vs. consumer/gender/title/etc.):

_____

_____

Where Research Is to Be Conducted:

_____

Supplier Expectations:

_____

Your Proposed Role:

_____

Schedule:

_____

Required Deliverables:

_____

Contact Information:

_____

Chapter 2 Take-Aways

☑ The Request for Proposal (RFP) should include:

- Brief background of the study.

- Key research objectives.

- "Sub" Objectives—"like to know" vs. "need to know" information.

- Timing for the project.

- Methodology being considered.

- Countries to include.

- Specifications for target respondents.

- Suggestions for sample sources.

- What you expect from the supplier.

- Your role in the research process.

- Required proposal format.

- Your available budget.

- Your contact information.

- Proposal submission instructions.

3

Selecting Vendors for International Research

Vendor selection varies when you venture abroad.

While many aspects of vendor selection for international research projects are similar to the planning involved for a domestic study, other issues also must be considered. If you are uncertain if something is important enough to mention, err on the side of caution and include it. Providing greater information in your request to the suppliers should ensure more details in the resulting proposals. Exhibit 3.1 is a checklist of key concerns you should be certain to address with potential vendors.

EXHIBIT 3.1
Vendor Characteristics

✔ Have you worked successfully on other projects with the vendor?

✔ Does it offer the necessary translation/ interpretation capabilities for your markets?

✔ Does it have experience in the markets/regions you will be conducting your study?

✔ Has it conducted research with the targets you will be addressing in the markets?

✔ Does it have access to the sample that will be needed for your study?

✔ Does it conduct the research from its own locations or does it subcontract any portion of it?

✔ What type of references has it provided you?

Past Experience

Have you worked successfully on other projects with the vendor? An obvious attraction to selecting one vendor over another would be having had a successful previous experience with that vendor in the past. If things went smoothly before, there is every reason to expect a good working relationship this time around. Still, it is always good to be open-minded about new vendors and to remember that things can change over time even within the best of firms. Check for any changes in its key staff, management and/or procedures: Any or all changes could potentially affect how your current project may be handled.

Furthermore, if your previous experiences with the supplier were solely domestic in scope, remember that international research projects generally require additional skill sets. Indeed, a new vendor that has experience in your industry or with the specific type of methodology you need this time, and/or the regions you plan to investigate in your study might be preferable to a familiar firm that is less qualified for this particular type of study.

Translation/Interpretation Capabilities

Does your vendor offer the necessary translation/interpretation capabilities for your markets?

You might ultimately select a German firm to conduct focus groups for you in Frankfurt, Germany, but the same firm may not be able to conduct similar focus groups in

Lyon, France, because they do not have access to a fluent French-speaking moderator.

Likewise, a qualified Mexican market research supplier may well be able to handle the nuances of dialects in various South American countries, but not have the interviewers available to conduct the same study in Portuguese in Brazil.

While your vendor may subcontract some portion of the interviewing, translation, moderating, etc, it is important to know *how* each vendor proposes to handle this aspect of the research.

Relevant Market Experience

Do the vendors have experience in the markets/regions you will be conducting your study in? While it is not necessary that the research vendors have physical offices in each country where you are planning to conduct your research, it is advisable to work with a vendor who actually has had experience conducting studies in these countries. They should have partners or preferred vendors with whom they frequently work in the proposed regions.

Their experience should save you from "recreating the wheel" in terms of selecting the most viable methodology, developing appropriate screener questionnaires, setting schedules and so on.

Furthermore, it will enable them to provide crucial

cultural insights that should help ensure that your study will be successful.

Familiarity with Target Markets

Has the vendor conducted research with the targets you will be addressing in the markets?

When conducting research abroad, it is important to recognize, as noted earlier, that accepted business practices as well as consumer habits are likely to vary from what you are familiar with in your home marketplace. Check with your potential vendors to see if they specialize in business-to-business research or consumer studies or are capable in both arenas. It certainly is possible for a firm to survey in both arenas, but you should request several examples of specific projects which they have conducted. Request several references and inquire as to how their interviewers are trained in terms of executive versus consumer interviewing. The tone of business and consumer interviews tend to vary dramatically, so you will want to ensure that your selected vendor is able to handle these different audiences over the course of your study. And check the references!

All vendors can purchase lists from list or database services. Some research suppliers, however, may have additional resources available to them, such as subscriptions with Dun & Bradstreet's service or perhaps their own proprietary panels of pre-screened respondents that they can use in your particular study.

Access to Appropriate Samples

Does the vendor have access to the sample that will be needed for your study?

"Sample" refers to the contact information (names, telephone numbers, email addresses and other related contact details) used to identify and screen potential survey respondents or focus group participants for your study.

Possible sample sources include:

- Customer lists
- Databases
- Panels
- Lists ordered from list brokers
- Periodical subscriber lists
- Membership directories

These sample sources may vary widely as indicated below.

Customer Lists

These are made up from your own sources of customer information from company records, product registration databases, sales executives' records, etc.

The more detailed and current these records, the better they will be for use as research samples. Often, however, registration databases leave much to be desired, because the customers must choose to self-register and thus there can be a bias as to the type of customer that will take the time necessary to do so.

Databases

Dun & Bradstreet is probably the most recognized name in terms of firms providing business databases. It maintains business details across the board, making it a preferred source for a business sample. Clients can buy subscriptions to these services, and often your vendor may have an existing subscription that can make it more cost-effective.

Panels

Panels are generally made up of consumers. They are set up and coordinated by research firms. Panel participants often receive incentives for their ongoing participation. Clients are able to target whom they want as panel members through the panel coordinating firm by specific demographic qualifiers.

While businesses are not generally as frequently represented in such panels, you may be able to target business respondents from consumer panels based on their responses to screening questions related to their professions and the industries in which they are employed. Also, a number of reputable research suppliers offer panels of, for example, information technology professionals.

Exhibit 3.2 provides information about a number of different research panel providers and how their panels are comprised.

EXHIBIT 3.2[1]
Global Online Panel Providers

- **GMI**—consumer and business, worldwide (450K households) *www.gmi-mr.com.*

- **Greenfield Online (includes Ciao)**—primarily consumer, worldwide with some specialized panels available *(i.e.,* automobile, healthcare, etc.) *www.greenfield.com.*

- **Novatris (part of Harris Interactive)**— primarily consumer, Europe (300K panelists in France, 140K in Italy, 51K in Germany and 25K in the UK); also has limited business panel *www.novatris.fr.*

- **eRewards**—consumer and business, US and Canada (1M consumers, 450K business professionals) *www.e-rewards.com.*

- **SSI**—primarily consumer, US, Canada and the UK (3.5M household members in the US, 100K in the UK and 50K in Canada *www.surveysampling.com.*

These represent only some of the key players in research panels. Other firms include Synovate (*www.synovate.com*), Acrobat Research (*www.acrobat-research.com*) and Decision Analyst Inc. (*www.decisionanalyst.com*).

Lists Ordered from List Brokers

In addition to the more familiar large-scale database providers, such as Dun & Bradstreet, literally thousands upon thousands of other firms offer to sell lists for use in sales and/or research efforts. For example, Alpha Marketing & Consulting (*www.internationallists.com*) and MarketScan (*www.marketscan.co.uk*) offer international lists that could potentially meet your research sampling requirements.

Be sure that whoever is responsible for obtaining the lists for your study checks the list company's credentials, their process for list compilation and the frequency with which the lists are updated or refreshed. Also confirm that the list company can provide the contact details in the format your methodology will require (i.e., email addresses, home or business telephone numbers, mailing address, demographic or firmographic pre-screened information, etc.).

Periodical Subscriber Lists

Certain periodicals may sell access to their subscriber lists, but remember that the subscribers themselves may, based on privacy law requirements, have opted out of being included in these lists. This, again, could potentially bias your sample. On the positive side, however, subscribers to specific periodicals may be an excellent match to the target market you are trying to reach. Therefore, they are worth consideration as a potential sample source.

One good example of this type of sampling is a project that involved surveying video/multimedia professionals, a highly specialized group that would take a long time to identify via a regular screening process. Exhibit 3.3 contains a list of periodicals offering lists that would meet the survey sample requirements in this instance.

Membership Directories

While lists of members of organizations, associations and the like usually provide fairly accurate and up-to-date contact information, they are not readily released for sales or research purposes. Membership groups carefully guard their members' privacy. Furthermore, there is some bias in such samples, if they are available at all, as you reach only those contacts that pay dues and not necessarily all who would be eligible for your study.

About lists in general: What might be considered to be a readily available list source to acquire in your home country could be extremely difficult to obtain in other countries. Privacy laws and call restrictions may also vary from country to country, making contacts much less easy to obtain. Your market research vendor should be able to

EXHIBIT 3.3
Periodicals List for Video/Multimedia Professionals

Video Systems

- Information is provided by types of equipment, job titles, etc. It will do an email "blast" to applicable subscribers to get them to the survey site.
- Its subscriber base consists of video professionals in independent production, business, broadcast and cable television, production/entertainment, government and nonprofit sectors.

"The Digital Studio Magazine"

- It has lists of subscribers available, but not by email addresses.
- Target audience consists of creative and technical experts who manage a creative or production staff and who specify, recommend or authorize the technology purchases needed in their workstations or studios. Approximately 25 percent of these individuals are executives, owners, principals or general managers of their companies. Other roles include digital video professionals, DVD authors, corporate video producers, in-store audio and video editors, post production service providers, and IT experts who maintain network performance and guide storage and infrastructure hardware and software purchasing decisions.

Digital Media

- It offers subscribers the opportunity to opt-in/opt-out of providing email addresses. Its available lists allow you to reach professionals in distinct market segments including broadcast and post production, streaming media, digital video, animation, special effects, desktop publishing, imaging and design, audio, CAD, workstations, game development and film productions.

address these issues and be able to suggest sample sources for your project.

About recruitment via the Internet: If your initial plan is to obtain your sample by recruiting participants or respondents via the Internet, you might be surprised to find that it is generally more difficult to do this outside of the United States. Not all global regions have Internet panels, nor do all populations, particularly among consumers, rely as heavily on the Internet as a communication tool and information source as do Americans.

Subcontracting

Does the vendor conduct the research or do they subcontract? Research vendors may subcontract one or more portions of studies for any number of reasons, including overcoming language barriers, better addressing time zones for interviewing times, the need to manage large numbers of interviews over a relatively short period of time and/or providing comfortable situations for respondents in terms of speaking with someone with whom they can better identify.

Subcontracting should not necessarily be considered to be a detriment to your project and, when the initiating lead vendor manages the process well, it can actually speed up the study and provide more accurate results. It is, however, very important to address precisely how your research supplier plans to manage any portion of the project in its own locations and what it will allocate to sub-contract. If they use subcontractors, they should demon-strate how they expect to maintain quality throughout the project. And, above all, it is important that the lead ven-dor provides you, the client, with a single point of contact to work with you throughout the project.

Types of References

Always ask your potential research suppliers to provide you with several professional references. These profes-sional references are a form of insurance for you, allow-ing you to validate that the vendors in question will be able to do what they promise they will do and that they are capable of doing it to your expectations.

Always contact the references that suppliers provide. Even with the obvious awareness that the vendors will only knowingly provide you with what they perceive to be excellent references, these contacts should still be able to give you a feel for where the vendors' strengths as well as their weaknesses are. This can be helpful in weighing your available options during your vendor selection process.

Chapter 3 Take-Aways

☑ Key considerations when considering potential vendors:

- Successful past experience with vendor
- Translation/interpretation capabilities offered in your markets
- Experience in the markets/regions research will be conducted in
- Research experience with the targeted respondents
- Access to the necessary sample
- Internal versus subcontracting of the research
- References

4

The Proposal Process

Once you have determined which market research suppliers appear to be the most suitable for your international project and you have your RFP prepared, you can begin the formal proposal process in earnest. This chapter focuses particularly on two components: getting the proposal out and evaluating the responses that come in.

Exhibit 4.1 shows a step-by-step guide to the components of the proposal process.

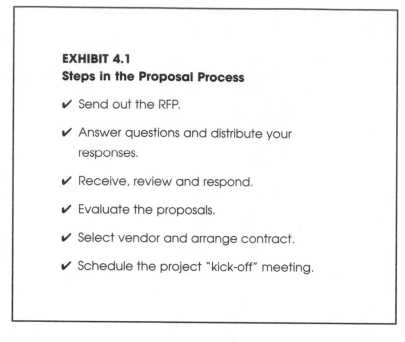

EXHIBIT 4.1
Steps in the Proposal Process

✔ Send out the RFP.

✔ Answer questions and distribute your responses.

✔ Receive, review and respond.

✔ Evaluate the proposals.

✔ Select vendor and arrange contract.

✔ Schedule the project "kick-off" meeting.

Detailed descriptions of how to assess and compare vendor proposals as well as some sample guidelines of each of these elements follows.

Sending Out the RFP

Because you will want to receive proposals as quickly as possible, you will want to get out your RFP quickly. The most efficient means of getting your RFP out to your selected vendor list is via email. This also allows you to flag your message with the RFP attached in order to confirm its receipt. Avoid sending all of the vendors on your RFP distribution list a single message. This will help you to maintain control over the bid process without dealing with the potential that vendors would communicate between and among themselves about their proposals.

If you are bidding the project to firms that would manage the overall study in all regions from a central location, you should plan to send the RFP to at least three vendors. If you are bidding the project *by separate* region (i.e., separate vendors for each region included in the study), you should send the RFP to several vendors *per* region. This allows you to ensure that you are obtaining the best value for your research budget and it also provides you with a variety of methodology options for the study.

In the not-so-uncommon situation that you do not have any specific research suppliers in mind, there are resources to assist you in identifying appropriate vendors. You can look to any or several of the following sources to identify qualified market research suppliers with international project experience:[1]

- *www.qrca.org* (QRCA)
- *www.marketingpower.com* (AMA)
- *www.mra-net.org* (MRA)
- *www.esomar.org* (ESOMAR)
- *www.greenbook.org* (AMA)
- *www.bluebook.org* (MRA)
- *www.quirks.com*
- Quirk's Marketing Research Review

Responding to Vendor Questions

The next step is to answer questions and distribute your responses to all vendors. Expect that bidding suppliers will have a wide range of questions regarding your RFP. You should have specified in your directions how and to whom these questions should be addressed.

To keep it fair, distribute each of your responses to all vendors without identifying the source of the question.

Once again, plan to handle this question-and-answer process via email as this will allow the process to move ahead at a faster pace than by playing "phone tag" across different time zones.

Examining Proposals

When you receive the proposals from the bidding suppliers, allow adequate time to read each of them *thoroughly*. Now is the time to ask any questions. They may be on any portion of the proposal. Some examples:

- Why have the vendors selected their recommended methodologies?
- Are the suggested sample sizes adequate (as well as feasible) for the regions included in the study?
- Are there anticipated issues with your requested schedule for the project?

As the old adage goes, "There are no stupid questions"! Clarifying details now can only yield positive results and give you the clearest possible picture of your options for the project.

Comparing the Proposals

The initial review of the proposals may have resulted in a narrowing down of your supplier options. Now, however, you need to compare the proposals themselves to determine the right research supplier (see the next section) and the most appropriate methodology (see Chapter 3).

The Decision Process

How do you decide on the right research supplier? Once you have received your requested proposals, you and your internal project team should review each of the proposals and select the most appropriate, best-qualified research supplier to meet the needs you have expressed. You must determine the strengths and weaknesses of each vendor based on the proposals they have provided you with. What is the best way to accomplish this rather daunting task?

There are several means by which you and/or your team can more easily evaluate the proposals. The first is the most basic: a subjective consideration of the proposals. In other words, consider what your intuition is telling you when you are reading through the proposals. Take into consideration not only the proposals themselves, but the overall experience you have had with each of these research suppliers *during* the proposal process. Look at both the positives and the negatives.

For example, on the positive side:

- Do you trust the vendors? Have you had any positive past experiences on other research studies using any of the vendors who have bid on your project?

- In speaking with the suppliers (or in reading their response to your requests) was there a willingness to disagree and suggest better ways of meeting your objectives? They didn't say "yes" just to pacify your team?

- Do the vendors express a willingness to work within your budget and, in fact, suggest cost-effective measures to do so?

- Are any of the vendors suggesting new ways or unique methodologies to help meet your objectives; in other words, thinking "outside of the box"?

From a negative perspective:

- Did you experience any significant misunderstandings during the proposal phase?

- Were there any vendors who simply "just did not get it" when interpreting your RFP?

- Do you feel that there are noticeable personality conflicts between you, your team members and any of the vendor contacts you dealt with during the proposal phase?
- Did any of the estimates seem significantly out of line, either extremely high or so low that they seemed too good to be true?

After you get past the more "emotional" aspects of the vendor selection, you should take an objective look at all of the proposals and conduct a detailed comparison of their strengths and weaknesses. One of the most effective means of comparing the proposals is to design a spreadsheet or matrix, which allows you to see side-by-side comparisons of what you determine are the key aspects of the proposals. Exhibit 4.2 is an example of such comparisons.

The elements of the proposals which are to be compared should include at least the following:

- Recommended methodology
- Grasp of the objectives
- Regions
- Suggested screening criteria
- Sample sizes and quota groups
- Sample sources
- Schedule
- Estimated cost

EXHIBIT 4.2 Decision Spreadsheet

Vendors Bidding:	ABC MARKET RESEARCH	QUALITY RESEARCH	RESEARCH INCORPORATED
Methodology	Telephone Survey	Focus groups followed by telephone survey (in-person surveys in China)	Web-based survey
Regions	US, UK, Germany, China	US, Germany, France, China	US, Germany, France, South Korea
Targeted Respondents	Consumers with cellular phones; ages 22–30 years	Consumers with cellular phones; ages 20–30 years	Consumers with cellular phones; ages 16–30 years
Sample Size	300 US/150 each in UK/Germany/China	4 groups per country/ 300 phone in US/150 each in other countries	400 US/200 each other country
Quota Groups	50/50 male/female	50/50 male/female; Split between 20–24 year-olds and 25–30 year-olds	50/50 male/female; Split between 16–18 year-olds; 19–23 year-olds and 24–30 year-olds
Sample Source	List broker	List broker and possible subscriber lists	Panel contacts
Proposed Schedule	Approximately 8 weeks from approval to report delivery	12 weeks from start to final report delivery with interim focus group report provided at 5 weeks	6 weeks from contract signing until presentation
Estimated Cost	$XX,XXX	$XXX,XXX	$XX,XXX

Elements of the Proposals

RECOMMENDED METHODOLOGIES

It is likely that one or all of the bidding suppliers will have different methodologies to recommend for your project. Unless the study is, for example, a clear-cut focus group project, you should take adequate time to review the vendors' various suggestions and their reasons for choosing these routes to get the information you need.

GRASPING THE OBJECTIVES

Do any of the vendors have a particularly good grasp of your objectives? Who is providing added background and suggestions that may prove helpful in the analysis and recommendation phases of the project?

REGIONS

Are all of the vendors who are bidding on this project capable of conducting the proposed research in the regions you requested in your RFP? Are reasons for any changes to the regions clearly explained?

And, given these changes, are they due to a supplier's inability to conduct the study in one or more of the regions which you requested in your RFP? Or are its suggested changes due to a research-related recommendation that is geared toward obtaining better results for you based on your stated objectives?

SUGGESTED SCREENING CRITERIA

How is the supplier suggesting that you identify the correct research respondents or focus group participants? Are they able to determine some of the qualifiers through the sample itself (i.e., by requesting certain professional titles, age groups, etc.)? What are their reasons for recommending specific screener questions and how will it ultimately improve your results by ensuring that you reach precisely the right contacts?

SAMPLE SIZES AND QUOTA GROUPS

Some basic questions include:

- How statistically reliable are the sample sizes which the research supplier is proposing for your study?
- How many focus groups are proposed and with how many participants in each?
- What is the reasoning behind the number of groups and the proposed participant profiles for each group? Will these produce the information you need to obtain?
- What type of cross-tabulations and analysis can you expect to be able to conduct based on results from a survey with the suggested sample size and how accurate will the results within each quota group be?

SAMPLE SOURCES

Samples for market research studies can be obtained from a variety of sources and they will differ in their reliability, business versus consumer lists, number of contacts available, the specifications by which you are able to break out the sample (i.e., age, gender, profession, educational background, income level, etc.).

SCHEDULE

Typical scheduling issues include:

- Which research supplier appears to be best able to meet your scheduling requirements?
- Are you being realistic in your expected timetable?
- Are the vendors being realistic about whether or not they can complete the study within the timeframe you requested?

Note that the starting and ending points defined by each vendor may be different. One may start from the kick-off meeting date while another may consider project start-up to be from the date the project is awarded to the vendor.

ESTIMATED COST

Be careful not to look just at the bottom-line cost on each proposal as your deciding factor when comparing the vendors' proposals. It is important to remember that their varying methodologies, recommended sample sizes and list sources may differ substantially and hence their costs may not directly comparable. It is best to look at all other aspects first and see what proposal you would select based on its research merit and how well it would meet your stated objectives and *then* review the budget implications.

Also be certain that you are comparing "apples to apples" in terms of costs: are all of the prices listed in the same currency? If, for example, one is in US dollars, another in Euros and another in Canadian dollars, you need to put them in the same currency figures to make your comparisons. You can certainly ask the bidding suppliers to convert the amounts for you, but if time is of the essence, you can do the conversions yourself at *http://www.oanda.com/convert/classic.*

Other Aspects of the Proposal

Other aspects of the proposals you should compare include:

- Translation capabilities/recommendations
- Moderator availability
- Quality control procedures

Translation Capabilities/Recommendations

If your study is going to require translations into one or more languages, be certain that the bidding suppliers have addressed how the translation process will be handled and what the expected costs will be. Bear in mind that these costs are generally based on an estimated length of your questionnaire and will vary based on the actual number of words once this is finalized.

Moderator Availability

Not all research suppliers have their own moderators on staff, particularly for projects that are international in scope. It is helpful to review focus group proposals in detail to determine how the vendors plan to handle this aspect of your research.

Look for consistency wherever possible. If they have experienced moderators in one or more countries on staff, reporting will be more consistent across the countries because they can more easily work together on evaluating the results of the groups. If they use one or more freelance moderators, choose a vendor who will manage this process and have one of its own managers handle the briefings and potentially also attend all of the sessions to ensure that the groups are conducted in a similar manner throughout all of the regions involved.

Quality Control Procedures

Quality control in the research process could lend itself to a book by itself.

For now, however, look for market research suppliers who stress quality in their proposals, not just that they "provide quality," but also *how* they provide it.

Quality crosses over into all areas of the project. Vendors should demonstrate how they intend to control quality in the project, including these areas:

- **Reviewing and testing the questionnaire design.**

  It is crucial that you and your team review the questionnaire and ask your supplier liaison if you are not certain that all of your objectives will be met given the questions being asked. Are the following (as applicable to your particular study) being covered?

  —Are closed-end questions providing adequate lists of potential responses as well as an "Other" option to accommodate unexpected responses?

  —Are all brands/product names, etc., included where they should be?

  —Is the introduction to the respondent clear and polite?

  —Is the wording of the questionnaire going to get answers that specifically relate to the objectives you have for the study?

  —Are the screening questions going to identify the proper respondents for the survey?

  These are just a few of the things you should be looking for, even if you are not heavily involved in the actual design of the questionnaire. Likewise, the project manager and your contact from the research supplier should also be asking these questions during the review of the survey instrument. It is also advisable to have an interviewer supervisor (for phone surveys) and the vendor's data processors review the questionnaire as well, in order to avoid any unforeseen issues once the survey is underway.

- **Back-translation process for materials requiring translation.**
  While this is mentioned in several places in this book, I cannot stress strongly enough the importance of the back-translation process. In order to obtain accurate data from respondents, you must ensure that the materials used in the research—everything from the questionnaire to advertising copy boards to self-completion exercises and so on—is readily comprehended by the research respondents. Translating the translation back into the original language is a meticulous test of the adequacy of the translation being used. How does the vendor propose to handle this?

- **Thorough briefings with interviewers, moderators and interpreters.**
  Your research supplier typically will be the one who conducts the briefings with any staff involved including those subcontracted to work on

your research project. Whenever possible, your presence during these initial briefings either in-person or via videoconference or teleconference, helps ensure that you and the vendor are on the "same page" in terms of what is to be done and during what timeline. All terminology with which the research staff is not familiar should be clarified at this time.

- **Pre-testing the questionnaire with actual respondents.**
  By pre-testing the questionnaire with actual respondents in a series of interviews (for example, 5 to 10 completed surveys), the research supplier will be able to identify early on any areas which need to be clarified or worded differently. Once the pre-test of the survey is completed, interviewing is usually put on hold until any issues which have come up are discussed with the client and corrected.

- **Monitoring interviews/recruitment efforts.**
  Interviewer supervisors and the research vendor's project manager will typically listen in on a certain percentage of interview calls to monitor both how well the interviewers are conducting the interview as well as how well the targeted respondents are comprehending what the questions are asking. Are they familiar with the terminology used? Do the

translations appear to be making sense or are respondents becoming somewhat confused over the course of the interview? This monitoring process allows problems with the questionnaire and/or other aspects of the study to be addressed quickly to keep the research on track.

- **Validation of completed surveys.**
  An interviewer supervisor is often asked to validate a certain percentage of the completed survey questionnaires. This is done by re-contacting a defined percentage of the research respondents and clarifying their responses or re-asking one or two questions to ensure that the interviewers are correctly recording responses and are indeed conducting the interviews they have recorded.

- **Review of the data tables.**
  Both the data processing staff and the project manager and/or research analyst should proof the resulting research database tables for your project. If something does not "add up," it could be an incorrect entry during data processing or a problem with the questionnaire itself. In either case, it is important to identify any potential discrepancies before the data is assumed to be correct and decisions are made on the client side.

- **Simple proofreading of all materials and reports.**

  This particular point seems so obvious, yet so often typographical errors or mistranslations occur in either the survey materials, focus group presentation boards and/or a research report, it is important to mention it. All materials, no matter how trivial they might seem, should be carefully proofread by more than one person as well as you whenever possible.

Simply put, quality control is a vital part of the research process. While you can, and without a doubt should, adhere to the preceding quality control measures, the main responsibility for quality control is in the hands of your selected research vendor. This is why it is so important to discuss vendors' quality control processes during the proposal phase of your research program.

Reporting Deliverables

Is one vendor offering more in terms of reporting? If the costs for one vendor seem excessive versus others who are bidding, it may be that the vendor is providing an estimated budget for a more complicated statistical analysis, model or program. Before you cross that one off of your list, first consider the value-added benefits from the proposed analysis. And, if you do not believe you require this additional reporting capability, consider asking the vendor to revise these costs accordingly. This will give you a better comparison between vendors.

Contact Point

Having a single point of contact for project management is key to the success of your research effort. Any vendor who provides a list of contacts for you may actually be doing you a disservice by adding complications to the process. Certainly, it is important that more than one person on the vendor side is always apprised and up-to-date on your project, but unless your key contact is on vacation, there is no reason for you to deal with multiple contacts.

You can visually conduct a comparison of the proposals or you can apply a point system to all or some of the key aspects of the proposals in order to develop a "score" for each proposal.

Other Aspects

Do not forget to consider other aspects of the proposals that may not really fit neatly into your spreadsheet such as the following.

Vendors' Timeliness

If one of the vendors responding to your RFP submits their proposal a day or two late, consider whether or not this could indicate how the vendor usually handles deadlines. On the other hand, if the vendor notified you of the expected delay and provided a reasonable explanation, then you might want view it differently.

The Experience of the Research Team

The experience of the research team assigned to your project can spell the difference between success and failure.

If a vendor is putting lower-level staff (i.e., interns, junior analysts or similar staff) on the proposed team for your research project, you may not receive the level of expertise you require. At the same time, you should also consider the possibility that the proposed staff is most likely capable and the fact that they are not upper management level staff may very well keep project management costs more in line with your budget.

The key here is to ask questions and be certain that you are completely satisfied with the vendors' responses. Consider conducting teleconferences with each of your bidding vendors' teams prior to making a final decision and awarding your project.

The Vendors' Experience

Which of the vendors being considered has experience with projects similar to yours? When determining which research suppliers to send your RFP to (see Chapter 2), I suggested that you look for those with past experience in similar projects that utilized the methodology they are recommending in their proposal. While this is not an absolute requirement, this added experience should be factored into your decision-making process when selecting the vendor to conduct your research study. Such previous experience will no doubt help your selected vendor to better design your study.

Vendor Familiarity with Your Industry and Markets

The greater a vendor's familiarity with research in your own industry and international markets, the easier the process. Keep this in mind when evaluating research suppliers bidding on your project.

Vendors' Communication Plans

Do any of the vendors propose a communication plan for the vendor/client relationship in their proposal? The best solution is a single contact where one key manager from the research supplier keeps you regularly apprised of the progress of the study across all regions being researched.

Example 4.1 shows a detailed proposal from a research supplier in response to a client's RFP.

Selecting Vendor and Arranging Contract

Whoever selects the vendor should be sure to consider all the inputs from internal team members who have reviewed the proposals. However, you have at the outset of the proposal process determined who has the final authority to select the vendor. The selection should not be allowed to become a political issue or a vendor popularity contest.

Once the vendor is selected, move quickly to complete

Example 4.1
SAMPLE RESEARCH PROPOSAL

XYZ TELECOMMUNICATIONS RESEARCH
123 MAIN STREET
ANYTOWN, NY USA
TELEPHONE: (123)456-7589
EMAIL: RESEARCH@XYZ.COM
WIRELESS PROGRAM POSITIONING STUDY

1. INTRODUCTION

ABC Wireless has developed a series of wireless service and payment plans targeted at different segments of the consumer marketplace based on perceived needs. The options consist of the following service/payment categories:

1. Basic—a no-frill plan designed solely for basic call activity with occasional voicemail requirements.
2. Teen Time—a plan targeted at the teen user segment with text messaging and 3-way calling capabilities along with extra minutes for low rates.
3. Advanced—a plan targeted to the busy adult consumer to simplify life in general—speed-dial, within family plan free calling, call reminders and voicemail with quick response options (i.e., ability to assign numbers to basic messages).
4. Jet-setters—a range of services targeted at customer needs among business travelers with specialized bill tracking services, call-waiting and high-end voicemail services.

A research project is required which will help validate the targeting and positioning of these service/payment plan offerings and provide insights that will help ABC Wireless to choose the plans and marketing strategies that will be most likely to maximize its market share.

2. RESEARCH OBJECTIVES

The objectives of the proposed project can be summarized under two main headings:

    a. to support ABC Wireless's tactical marketing by validating and refining the targeting of current service/payment plan offerings—identifying, through analytical research, how to achieve the best match between service characteristics and the related costs and customer segments driven by needs.

    b. to support program development by validating and refining the services that need to be incorporated into each payment plan in order to win competitive share (*e.g.*, which are the features that determine or drive competitive share and which are features that are contributing little to choice and might potentially be dropped from the plan thereby cutting ABC's costs.

3. SCOPE OF PROJECT

The project is to be conducted in the US, the U.K. and Germany and only among current users and intending first time purchasers of wireless phone plans in the broad consumer marketplace who would personally make the choice of product for their next purchase.

4. RECOMMENDED APPROACH

When customers buy services such as wireless plans for their cellular phones, their purchase decision process involves a balancing of a number of different elements in the overall choice—service features, wireless service brand, past experience with wire services and its reputation and price. In order to meet the research objectives, a methodology is required which will simulate the way these elements are balanced or "traded off" so that needs and priorities can be identified and matched to other demographic and lifestyle information to create distinctive customer segments. These can then be addressed both in respect of current service/price offerings and in respect of future product offerings optimised to the needs and priorities of each segment.

Because of the enormously large number of potential choices or trade-offs which a customer has potentially to make in the purchase choice, structured research methodologies typically involving both a data collection process/vehicle and an analytical model/simulator have been developed to rationalize the research process and make it acceptable and comprehensible to survey respondents. Of the different market research tools and methodologies available, XYZ Telecommunications Research believes the best option is a technique called ShareSim® Simalto.

ShareSim® Simalto—An Overview

ShareSim® Simalto is an extremely flexible primary research-based methodology for analyzing and predicting customer wants, needs, and preferences in complex decision/choice situations where conventional survey techniques are inadequate. It is a proven and successful tool for matching a client's products, service and image as closely as possible with customer priorities and values in order to maximise market share potential, get the best return on investment, and increase customer loyalty and preference.

5. DATA COLLECTION AND SAMPLE DESIGN
Data Collection Method

Because of the highly visual nature of the ShareSim® Simalto data collection process, in which respondents are able to see the full implications of the "trade-offs" and prioritizations they make as they work through the question sequence, the methodology was originally designed for face-to-face administration. However, a Web-enabled version of the data collection process has now been developed which facilitates online self-completion by respondents in a managed sequence which mimics the interviewer-administered process.[2]

Recommended Sample Size

The ShareSim® Simalto methodology has been shown to be highly reliable and stable even at comparatively limited sample sizes. The optimal size and structure of the sample is therefore essentially a function of the degree of segmentation desired to use for survey control purposes rather than the overall size and structure of the universe. It is more important to have a sufficient sample of each designated segment than it is for each segment to have a sample size proportionate to its importance in the marketplace.[3]

6. REPORTING DELIVERABLE

Our budget assumes the following levels of reporting:

- **Management Presentation**—an in-person seminar-style presentation in a high-impact PowerPoint presentation format intended to stimulate questions and discussion as well as convey the findings and conclusions of the research.
- **Final Report**—a technical report consisting of relevant raw data sets demonstrating the build up of customer preferences and trade-offs, segmentations, and program optimization scenarios run by the XYZ project team.
- **Data Tabulations and/or data file**—the online model incorporates the ability to run a variety of data tabulations including conventional cross tabulations. XYZ Telecommunications will train ABC Wireless internal esearch staff and management members to work with this model so that future information needs related to this study can be met immediately as they arise.

Logistics
Project Management and Resourcing

XYZ Telecommunications Research sets up teams to manage and conduct projects on the following basis:

- **Account Executive**—responsible to the client for the quality, integrity and timeliness of the project and providing overall direction to the rest of the project team, including contribution to and sign off on the final report and presentation.
- **Project Manager**—responsible for day-to-day management of the project, including development of questionnaires, controlling samples and sampling procedures, interviewing schedules and interviewer/subcontractor management, leading the analysis process, and drafting of reports and presentations.
- **Project Analysts**—staff members who undertake secondary research, interviewing, and analysis tasks under the direction of the Project Manager.

- **Fieldwork Subcontractors**—XYZ Telecommunications Research buys fieldwork services outside of the US on a subcontract basis which allows us to choose the field partner(s) best suited to the requirements of individual projects.

Key project team personnel will be confirmed for ABC Wireless at the time of project commission. Biographies of the team members assigned to this project will be provided to the client at that time.

Briefing and Ongoing Quality Control

XYZ Telecommunications Research adheres to a strict quality control procedure for managing quantitative and field-based projects. Our briefing and quality control processes include:

a. A kick-off and background briefing meeting will be held with the client either in-person or via teleconference, prior to project set-up to:

- confirm the objectives, scope and methodology for the project and agree to or establish a procedure for agreeing to details of sample frames, etc.
- establish an agreed project timescale and key milestones (including deliverables such as sample frames and questionnaire/screener inputs required from the client team).
- agree to liaison and progress reporting procedures.

b. Wherever possible we will pre-test all survey questionnaires to ensure that respondent comprehension, question sequencing and routing and interview length are acceptable.

c. We will be in contact with the fieldwork agency(ies) on a regular basis to check on progress.

7. TIMETABLE

We estimate that an elapsed time of approximately 45 to 50 business days (9–10 weeks) will be needed to set up, conduct, and report the project as a whole to presentation. This overall timeline is made up of the following expected project tasks and target dates:

Project Tasks	Number of days:
Initial set up and team briefing	8–10
Obtaining and preparing sample frame(s)	
Drafting/finalizing questionnaire(s)/translations	
Briefing field team(s)/piloting	4–5
Main fieldwork	15–20
Data preparation/data processing	5
Executive analysis and drafting of presentation	7–9
Final reporting	5

A detailed schedule for the project will be presented for agreement after commission. The following target milestones for deliverables required from ABC Wireless will be critical to the timetable once the schedule is finally agreed:

- Kick-off meeting
- Completion and agreement of the service/pricing plan value and brand profiling grids
- Sign off of questionnaire(s)

While there may be some limited scope for flexibility, we reserve the right to submit a revised timetable if agreed deadlines are to be missed by more than five working days.

8. PROJECT COST

The project as set out in this proposal would cost $xxx,xxx.[4]

The project cost is made up of the elements outlined below.

	$
Meetings and Client Meetings	x,xxx
Project Set-up and Management	xx,xxx
Quantitative fieldwork program (inc respondent incentive)	xx,xxx
Data Processing (inc ShareSim model building and licence)	xx,xxx
Executive analysis and reporting	x,xxx
Other direct costs	x,xxx
Total Cost	**xxx,xxx**

The above is a firm and fixed price for conducting the project as specified in this proposal and is subject to the following assumptions and conditions:

a. The total cost includes provision for incentive payments for respondents.

b. Other direct costs include printing and copying; telephone costs (those not included in fieldwork charges); library and secondary research charges; purchase of sample frames; purchase of special materials needed to perform the research to be covered at cost plus a handling fee to be agreed upon.

Invoicing of fees would be on the following basis:

On commission of project	40%
On completion of fieldwork (after approximately 5 weeks)	30%
On completion of project	30%

9. CREDENTIALS AND RELEVANT EXPERIENCE[5]

This section would typically consist of the following information:

- The research supplier's history summarized to provide highlights that focus on experience key to the proposed project
- Brief biographies of the key team members proposed to work on this specific research project (unless these are not yet designated)
- Examples, possibly in the form of summarized case studies, of similar projects (in terms of industry, methodology, countries, etc.) which the research supplier has conducted
- Client references and contact information; these will not necessarily include references from within the same industry to avoid confidentiality conflicts
- Any specific details regarding specialized expertise which the vendor has in the areas of international research, analysis, etc.

any agreed-upon paperwork, such as a contract, purchase order and/or non-disclosure agreements.

Example 4.2 provides a sample of a research supplier contract for an international vendor.

The Kick-Off Meeting

The next step is to schedule the project "kick-off" meeting. It should be scheduled as quickly as possible following the signing of the contract, the purchase order release or whatever occurrence signifies the actual start of the project with the vendor. The meeting is the important start-up of the project and usually includes all of the active project team members from both the client and supplier sides. Chapter 8 provides a detailed guide for this meeting.

Example 4.2
THE RESEARCH COMPANY, INC.
TERMS & CONDITIONS OF BUSINESS

In these terms and conditions (except where the context otherwise requires) the following words shall have the following meanings:

"the Client"	the person, firm or company who contracts with the Company in this Agreement
"the Company"	The Research Company, Inc.
"MRS Code of Conduct"	The Code of Conduct for Market Research published from time to time by the UK Market Research Society (*www.mrs.org.uk*)
"Project"	the Project specified in the Proposal including any extension or variation which is agreed in writing with the Company

"Project Team"	employees of the Company and its contractors (if any) working on the Project
"the Proposal"	the proposal document prepared by the Company prescribing its proposed Services in detail
"Quotation"	the fees quoted for the Project, as set out in the Proposal
"Services"	research, design and services as set out in the Proposal
"Terms"	these terms and conditions

1. General

1.1 The preparation of the Proposal and the performance of the Project by the Company are subject to the Terms laid out below. The Client acknowledges that it has received a copy of the Terms together with the Proposal. Acceptance by the Client of the Proposal is deemed to include acceptance of the Terms in their entirety unless otherwise specified in advance and agreed in writing by a Director of the Company.

1.2 No variation of the contract between the Client and the Company shall be effective unless and until confirmed in writing by a Director on behalf of the Company.

1.3 The Company will abide by the MRS Code of Conduct, a copy of which can be obtained upon request. Acceptance by the Client of the Proposal is deemed to include an obligation on the part of the Client to comply with the MRS Code of Conduct.

1.4 If during the development of the Proposal or the Project, the Client becomes aware or has reasonable cause to suspect there is any omission or inaccuracy in any assumption made by the Company it shall inform the Company forthwith, in writing. It is the responsibility of the Client to check assumptions made by the Company, and if attention is not drawn to any omission or inaccuracy in the assumption, that assumption shall be deemed to apply for the purpose of the Project.

1.5 While the Company will endeavour to use the project team specified in the proposal it retains the right to use other persons as it considers appropriate, including subcontractors.

2. Fees

2.1 Any Quotation is valid for two months from the date of submission to the Client, after which time the Company reserves the right to withdraw or revise the Quotation.

2.2 The fees quoted are for the Services as set out in the Proposal. The Company reserves the right to levy additional fees:

- If the assumptions by the Company detailed in the Proposal as having been used to produce the costing are found to have material omissions or inaccuracies.
- If the information provided by the Client is found to be misleading or inaccurate.
- If the Client requests changes to the Project or its scale, which result in higher costs being incurred.
- If failure or delay by the Client, in fulfilling its obligations, imposes additional costs on the Company.
- For Projects involving currencies other than sterling, where Quotations are subject to exchange rate movements between Quotation and delivery.

Should it be necessary to levy additional fees, the Company shall advise the Client as soon as is reasonably practical and give the Client the option to revise or terminate the Project, by notice in writing should it wish to do so.

2.3 In the event of a cancellation or postponement of the Project once commissioned, a charge will be made by the Company to cover fees on all work undertaken and the cost of all binding commitments entered into prior to the receipt of written notification.

2.4 In the event that the performance of the Project is rendered impossible or has to be deferred due to force majeure, the Company will endeavour to consult the Client as to whether the Project should be cancelled, postponed, or modified; but the Company reserves the right to take the final decision as to how to act in these circumstances. If cancelled, the Company shall be entitled to be paid all fees and costs already incurred or committed; if postponed or modified, the Company shall be entitled to revise the Quotation in which event the Client shall have seven days in which to accept or reject such revised Quotation; in the event of the Client rejecting such revised Quotation, the Company shall be entitled to terminate the Project by notice in writing.

2.5 Unless otherwise stated, the cost outlined in the proposal is inclusive of three copies of the final reporting documents. Any additional copies will be subject to a supplementary charge, which will be notified to the Client in advance, in writing.

2.6 Unless otherwise specified, fees are exclusive of VAT and, where appropriate, will be subject to the addition of VAT at the prevailing rate.

2.7 Unless otherwise agreed, fees will be invoiced as to 50% on acceptance of the Proposal, 25% on completion of fieldwork and 25% on submission of the final reporting documentation. The Company reserves the right not to commence work on the Project until written acceptance of the Proposal or a purchase order for the work is received from the Client, and the initial instalment of the costs is received. The Company also reserves the right not to deliver data, findings or reporting documents until at least 75% of the Project fees have been received.

2.8 All invoices are due for payment in full within 30 days of the invoice date. The Company reserves the right to charge interest at 5% per annum above the prevailing Bank of Scotland Base Rate on all overdue amounts. Interest will be calculated on a daily basis until payment and will be added to the outstanding amount without further notice or warning.

3. Confidentiality

3.1 The parties have imparted and may from time to time impart to each other certain confidential information relating to the Proposal or Project.

3.2 Each party agrees that it shall use such confidential information solely for the purposes of this agreement and that it shall not disclose directly or indirectly to any third party such information.

3.3 Unless given written permission to the contrary, the identity of the Client, the results of the Project, or any information obtained in confidence regarding the business of the Client shall, except as referred to below, remain confidential to the Company, its employees and any subcontractors of the Company.

3.4 The Company shall not disclose the identity of any respondent contacted during the research to any third party, including the Client, and shall not attribute any information collected to any particular individual or company unless given express permission to do so by the individual or company concerned, and in any event subject to the provisions of the Data Protection Act 1998.

3.5 Reports and other records provided by the Company are normally for use within the Client's Organisation or those of its consultants, and only on the Client's business. If wider circulation of results is intended, the Company's name may not be quoted in connection with the study until the exact form of any communication has been agreed by the Company. The Client undertakes to inform the Company of any intended wider publication prior to release and to offer identification of the Company as the supplier of the work to be published.

3.6 The Company may seek and the Client shall not unreasonably withhold permission to publicise the broad nature of the assignment and the Company's involvement, always providing that the Client's identity and the nature and detail of Project findings are kept confidential.

4. Rights of Ownership

4.1 Copyright in the Proposals remain the property of the Company.

4.2 All other written and electronic records of a Project, including questionnaires and working papers remain the property of the Company, who has the right to destroy these documents after a period of two years from the Project's completion without reference to the Client.

4.3 Upon payment of all fees and expenses due in respect of the Project, the Project results and all information and reporting provided to the Client by the Company, shall become the property of the Client.

5. Liability

5.1 The Client shall indemnify the Company against all claims, proceedings and liabilities (whether civil or criminal) of any kind whatsoever which may arise in consequence of the use, demonstration or consumption by any person of any goods or services supplied by the Client (or the Client's servants or agents) for the purposes of the Project, and against all legal costs, fees and expenses incurred by the Company in relation to any such claims, proceedings or liabilities.

5.2 Any results, prognoses, conclusions, recommendations and advice contained in any report or presentation are the result of careful analysis of the data. However, such data is based on small sample tests obtained by the Company and the Client acknowledges that such samples merely provide an indication, not a guarantee of the Company's findings. Accordingly, such reports and presentations are subject to the usual "statistical norms and variables" applied to research of this nature.

5.3 In translating survey results from the controlled test environment to the real market place it is possible that some of the assumptions on which the report is based will not remain constant. Any subsequent change in market conditions, or to the test product/service itself, could impact the initial performance predictions including possible invalidation of the results. Further, as the results are just one factor to be taken into account by the Client, the Client accepts that the Company cannot be liable for the consequences of any action based on the report or its interpretation.

5.4 The Company's total liability in contract, tort, including negligence and breach of statutory duty, misrepresentation or otherwise, arising in connection with the performance or contemplated performance of the Services shall be limited to the amount of the fees paid by the Client to the Company in respect of the Project.

5.5 The Company shall not be liable to the Client for any indirect or consequential loss or damage (whether for loss of profit, loss of business, depletion of goodwill or otherwise), costs or expenses which arise out of or in connection with the Project.

5.6 The Company cannot be held liable for any loss or damage resulting from adjustment to timings stated within the Quotation in carrying out the Services.

5.7 The Company shall owe no duty of care in respect of the Project or the results of the Project to any party other than the Client. The

Client shall not be entitled to assign the benefit of the Project or its results or the advice given by the Company.

6. Force Majeure

6.1 In these terms, "force majeure" shall mean any cause preventing either party from performing any or all of its obligations which arises from or is attributable to acts, events, omissions, or accident beyond the reasonable control of either party so prevented including without limitation strikes, lock-outs or other industrial disputes (whether involving the workforce of the party so prevented or of any other party), act of God, war, riot, civil commotion, malicious damage, compliance with any law or government order, rule, regulation or direction, accident, breakdown of machinery, fire, flood, storm or default of suppliers or sub-contractors.

7. Jurisdiction and Applicable Law

7.1 The Client agrees to submit to the exclusive jurisdiction of the English Courts in relation to any matter relating to or arising out of these Terms and the application and interpretation of these Terms shall be governed by English Law.

Chapter 4 Take-Aways

☑ The Proposal Process

- Send the Request for Proposal out

- Answer vendor questions

- Review proposals and ask questions

- Evaluate the proposals

- Select vendor and arrange contract

- Schedule the project "kick-off" meeting

☑ Selecting the Research Supplier

- Subjective review of proposals (intuition)
- Objective review of proposals (spreadsheet or matrix)
  - —Recommended methodology
  - —Regions
  - —Suggested screening criteria
  - —Sample sizes and quota groups
  - —Sample source
  - —Schedule
  - —Estimated cost
  - —Translation capabilities
  - —Moderator availability
  - —Quality control procedures
  - —Report deliverables
  - —Single point of contact on supplier team
  - —Timeliness of response to RFP
  - —Experience of supplier research team
  - —Past experience with similar projects
  - —Familiarity with your industry and markets
  - —Communications plan for study updates

5

What Type of Research Works Where?

Selecting Appropriate Methodologies

Certain methodologies work better than others, depending on where you plan to conduct your project. While your vendor may conduct a telephone survey in the United States and Western Europe, in Asian countries the interviews may be conducted face-to-face. Your research process must take into consideration the culture, societal norms, and business practices in all of the various countries where you plan to conduct your study.

While the *process* by which the survey is conducted may need to vary in different regions, the specific questions and the manner in which they are asked need to remain the same. This is necessary to permit correct analysis of the resulting data; otherwise you risk falling into the "comparing apples to oranges" scenario. The following are some examples of some "right" and "wrong" ways to get the job done.

Telephone Interviewing

For a long time phone interviewing was considered a staple tool of market researchers. Of course it is only effective if telephones are actually available to the potential respondents. In China and India, quantitative *consumer* studies are still better accomplished face-to-face. Given the local labor costs in these markets, it is surprisingly inexpensive to use this method, and you are far more likely to be able to reach your completion quotas. Alternatively, if you were to try reaching consumers in their homes for face-to-face research interviews (i.e., in Scandinavia or the US), you would risk rejection because they are less willing to open their doors to strangers, let alone provide them with personal information or opinions.

Detailed translation of your questionnaire is particularly crucial in *all* markets where the study is being conducted. You cannot expect that the telephone interviewers will be qualified interpreters as well! Furthermore, using native speakers as interviewers is more likely to increase your survey completion rates as they will be able to better comprehend responses to questions and probe for details with much greater ease.

In-depth Interviewing

Interviewing business contacts in Germany requires a great deal of finesse. Businesses (and, indeed, often individual consumers) are very protective of their privacy and are wary about providing surnames, business names, financial information and so forth. The country's privacy laws further promote this attitude. To go on-site to conduct face–to-face interviews at their workplace is difficult to arrange because interviewees need permission from high-level managers and assurance that they will be able to limit what you can see. For example, if you are planning to follow them for an hour to view workflow processes and so on, it may be more effective to solicit their input via a Web survey.

Managers in other countries are generally more receptive toward the in-depth interviewing process, but they are also becoming much more research "savvy." They expect to receive a substantial incentive for their time and inputs. Another word of caution: Check the legalities of offering cash (or other) incentive payments in the

115

countries in which you are conducting your research. Certain tax laws may prohibit such cash payments directly to constituents, in which case gifts or charitable donations may be more appropriate substitutes.

Focus Groups

Focus groups continue to be globally accepted as a means of testing concepts, messaging and a wide range of other objectives. They are, however, naturally subject to the limitations of the cultural norms of the regions in which they are conducted. Additional challenges arise because both verbal and nonverbal responses and reactions during the discussions may carry varying levels of significance among different cultures. This phenomenon is fraught with the potential for misinterpretation if this is not taken into consideration.

In Japan, for example, a Japanese moderator will frequently ask each participant in a group for their opinion or response on each item from the discussion guide. It is more a matter of listing individual responses than a group debate and/or discussion of a given topic. To add to these difficulties, the courteous Japanese do not like to directly challenge an issue or give a negative response regarding the product or subject being discussed. They generally will want to please their research "hosts" and, at the same time, attempt to agree with all comments being made by their counterparts in the focus group situation. Results, therefore, become blurred by the general polite optimism of the group comments. One-on-one personal interviews may prove more effective as you remove the societal constraints of the group situation.

In one such instance, I was viewing focus groups in Japan with several members of the client team. The Japanese moderator showed a sample product to the group, and one gentleman remarked that he liked it and explained why very briefly. When the moderator asked for other comments, all that she was able to elicit was complete agreement with the initial respondent's comments. While all of them might, of course, *really have agreed* with him on that item, this was the general tone throughout the group. Don't expect to receive a great deal of detail even if the response to the subject is genuinely positive.

Likewise, in Europe, you cannot "jump right in" and address your participants on a familiar, first-name basis. The warm-up period, with the expected courtesies honored, takes a bit longer than in the more relaxed atmosphere of groups in the United States. And you should also be sensitive to your audience's cultural and religious affiliations. For instance, in the Middle East, a female moderator would not likely be well received and would be viewed as stepping outside of her expected role in society.

And, along the same line of thought, how acceptable are the materials you may be planning to show and/or test during your focus group sessions? You should remain cognizant of your audience at all times to avoid committing a social *faux pas* that could reflect negatively on your company and its image.

If you are planning for the vendor to show advertisements, exhibit new product prototypes, etc., be aware that these materials need to be sent to the vendor in advance of the group meetings. While this may result in issues with customs officials, you can alleviate this by advance planning with your vendor. Be prepared to bring back-up materials, if feasible.

As with depth interview incentives, there can also be issues related to incentives for focus group participants. Different countries may have specific regulations and tax implications related to offering cash incentives or prize drawings. Your vendor should be able to assist you regarding these issues, but do not neglect to discuss this, as it is very important.

Web Surveys

Web surveys can also be a challenge depending on where you decide to conduct them. For example, while 63.9% of the United States population[1] has Internet access, in Latin America, the percentage of Internet users typically falls more into the 12% to 30% range. And in Asia, it can range from China with 7.8% having Internet access to South Korea, which boasts 74% of its population being connected. This obviously has an effect on how easy or difficult it will be to conduct a Web survey in these different markets. On the other hand, if your target group profile includes Internet users, a low percentage may not be a problem. Also, consider that Internet users may or may not be geographically clustered and may or may not share the same characteristics.

In addition, Web surveys require a very high-quality translation effort because a research interviewer is not available to clarify wording or concepts with the survey respondents. On the positive side, however, this methodology does allow for easier presentation of advertising tests, product photos, and so on and allows for some additional clarification not readily available via telephone interviews without prior mailing or faxing of the materials.

Mail Surveys

Mail surveys are less frequently used in international market research, but they can be appropriate when a Web survey or a telephone survey will not adequately cover all of the countries you are attempting to examine. In such cases, this is one possible methodology option, but it generally will generate very low response rates and therefore will give you far less control over your required quota groups. And, while you can provide print materials for review, it is not as secure an alternative as with a Web survey in terms of controlling the materials.

Obviously, mail surveys also require detailed

translations for each region included in a given research study. And remember that even more so than with surveys conducted by interviewers, your mail survey respondent is dependent on an accurate translation to get your point across. Respondents do not have the benefit of someone being there to explain the intended question's meaning or to define the terminology you use (for example, rating scales).

Another factor is the reliability and extent of the mail delivery system. In many countries of the former Soviet Republic, for example, mail delivery to homes or boxes is not quite yet a norm.

Diaries

Diary exercises are used to obtain a broad picture of how a consumer or a business person operates on a daily basis with respect to a certain product, process or task. The care respondents take in completing this type of research exercise is also likely to vary from country to country. In the US, diary entries may be less frequent and perhaps a bit haphazard. In Germany, on the other hand, great care will be taken to provide all possible details and meet all of the requested requirements of the exercise.

Regardless of the willingness of certain cultures to adhere to the diary process, the tedious and often repetitive nature of this task makes it a less frequently selected methodology. Also, this particular methodology requires a good deal of translation work following the completed exercise, as all entries must be translated for analysis.

Mystery Shopping

Mystery shopping remains a popular methodology particularly for consumer studies. It involves trained "interviewer/shoppers" shopping at a location, on the phone or via the Internet to review product promotions, sales and service techniques, pricing, etc., in a number of industries. This can, however, be much more difficult to implement when a number of different countries are included in the study, as the entire experience may vary from country to country in terms of how promotions occur, what expectations are in terms of sales and service efforts, and so on.

Coordinating mystery shopping programs with retailers in other countries can require finesse as well. An experienced vendor in the region will be needed to make the necessary arrangements; and, even then, be prepared to be involved throughout the project as instructions can be very detailed for these types of studies.

For example, in a Latin American mystery shopping study that involved business supply purchases, a number of issues had to be dealt with, particularly with regards to the following:

- Training the shoppers: Good survey interviewers are not necessarily good mystery "shoppers."
- Translation issues related to specific products that the shoppers were required to purchase.
- Completion of the shoppers' written evaluation forms.
- Where purchased products were to be delivered following the "shops."

And, despite the detailed advance preparations, problems still occurred. The "shoppers" were familiar with in-person interviews, but they were not used to having to follow through an entire purchase process themselves. As a result, they did not always purchase the product(s) that their project scenario required and the related evaluation forms were therefore also incorrect. It is difficult enough to explain such procedures in one's native language, so extra care is required when implementing this type of study abroad.

Chapter 5 Take-Aways

☑ Select the appropriate methodology considering:
  - Research objectives
  - Regions and target audience

☑ Choose what will work best:
  - Telephone interviewing
  - In-depth interviewing
  - Focus groups
  - Web surveys
  - Mail surveys
  - Diaries
  - Mystery shopping

6

Cultural Issues

You need to consider a wide range of cultural issues when undertaking a research project abroad. We have discussed methodologies and will address potential issues related to language barriers in the next chapter. Other cultural differences exist, however, that may take you by surprise over the course of your study. These differences affect the market research study itself in terms of the most appropriate methodology to use in a specific market. They also affect respondents' reactions and responses to certain types of questions or discussion of certain topics.

Rating Scales

One such example of how cultural differences affect research is that questions requiring numerical ratings on a scale (e.g., "rate this from 1 to 5") may ultimately cause confusion in the analysis of results. Different cultures will view a numerical scale from very different perspectives. Some will view a "3" on a scale of 1 to 5 as "good" rather than "average" or "fair," but others in different cultures will feel uncomfortable giving such a "low" rating because they want to avoid offending the survey sponsor. You should first and foremost seek advice from your suppliers, particularly those with local offices in the regions where the research is being conducted, to identify cultural issues that may affect your project.

Focus Groups

Focus group situations provide excellent examples of cultural variations. In some countries (with France and Germany coming to mind first), it is considered perfectly acceptable for the facility to provide alcoholic beverages to participants *during* the discussion groups. Furthermore, in France, participants may expect to be allowed to smoke cigarettes during their sessions.

In many European facilities, you will find the focus group room to be arranged more like a lounge area, with sofas and comfortable armchairs. Then you leave this setting only to arrive for a series of Asian groups and find that the focus group viewing window is only the size of your notebook.

In India, if you mention an incentive during the screening process, as is typically done in most Western research projects, you may actually have an adverse effect on your results. Focus group respondents in India will respond with what they believe you want to hear versus what they actually think about the topic or product. They feel this is necessary in order to reciprocate for the "monetary gift" you are providing.

And in the "creature comfort department": When you have focus groups anywhere in Europe, do not expect ice to be served in your beverages at the research facilities. Ice is not generally served in drinks, so if you are unaccustomed to beverages without it, be sure to request it several days in advance. During one series of focus groups I attended in Frankfurt, Germany, our research facility manager rushed to meet our American "need" for ice by sending an employee running down the street immediately before the groups met in order to purchase ice at a local McDonald's.

However, in Europe, what is missing in terms of ice is often made up for in terms of client food service in the viewing room. In France, you might actually enjoy full gourmet meals delivered to you and your colleagues in the focus group client viewing room during evening groups—a far cry from the dishes filled with chocolate candy and mixed nuts provided for clients in typical US facilities! Then when your focus group study takes you to China, you could end up being served western-style fast food as your supplier will strive diligently to make you feel at home.

Interactions between group participants are also likely to vary from country to country due to the room arrangements. In London, focus groups are often conducted in a casual "living room" type of setting, with respondents seated on sofas and stuffed easy chairs. Alternatively, Japanese focus group facilities are more inclined to favor round tables for group discussions rather than the oval or rectangular tables more commonly used in Western focus group situations.

This is a typical representation of the Japanese attitude regarding group interaction, wherein no one wants to "stand out" or to be accorded special status or, as noted earlier, appear to be discourteous by voicing their opposition to any of the other participants' ideas or comments in a public setting such as a focus group.

Furthermore, in Asian countries, you will typically encounter less personal space expectations for each individual. They have smaller personal space "bubbles" born of necessity and experience because of greater population density.

Alternatively, Italian focus groups are not run on a strict schedule. Participants often are very open and do not appreciate a "stop-watch" approach to their discussions, which may tend to be comparatively very emotional in their tone.

In some cultures, in the Middle East for example, it more than likely will be considered very inappropriate for a male interviewer to conduct an interview with a female respondent or for a female focus group moderator to conduct groups with male participants. Further difficulties might also occur in situations where focus groups might normally consist of mixed gender participants. Other religious or social taboos may also prevail.

Socioeconomic class can also play a role in the results of a research study. In India, for instance, distinctions between castes, genders, occupations, income levels and educational background should be carefully considered in the recruitment of participants for focus groups. If participants from dissimilar social backgrounds are combined in groups, the results will not accurately reflect the category you intend to study, nor is there likely to be comfortable interaction between group participants.

Business Practices

There are gender issues in many countries. Be on the "safe side" when dealing directly with a market research supplier abroad. In India, for example, avoid initiating hand shaking with female employees, as this is considered forward and unacceptable.[1]

Furthermore, expected professional behaviors, nuances in management practices, and so on can also play a significant role in the ultimate success of the project. Styles of project management will also vary from region to region. One such example is in Latin American countries. There you may find that your research suppliers have a much lower sense of urgency than you might expect from your project team overall. Schedules may lapse by a few (or more) days on occasion, or decisions may seem to take a good deal longer in the finalization, not because of a lack of interest or concern or poor management, but rather because of the culture's much more relaxed pace of life and the desire to develop a relationship with you before conducting business. The concept "time is money" doesn't work very well.

In addition to the more relaxed approach to task deadlines, in Mexico there are added delays in interviewing due to the two-hour, mid-day breaks when offices are typically closed and consumers are generally unavailable for surveying (though this is gradually changing). Be prepared for—even expect—such situations in this region in order to save yourself a good deal of stress.

And, of course, do not forget that other countries have different religious and public holidays than you do in your home country. These dates should also be taken into consideration when scheduling your fieldwork and focus groups. Disregarding these dates is likely to result in low group attendance rates and/or rather offended and stressed facility staff members. Likewise, you should also be certain to check with your local research supplier about other potential conflicts that could negatively affect your fieldwork schedule.

Major soccer matches in Europe, for example, will certainly take precedence over your research. Typically southern Europeans, particularly in France and Italy, take the entire month of August off as holiday time, rendering research attempts ineffective during that time period. And, in Brazil, you must avoid scheduling any research projects during February as they would likely be upstaged by Carnival.

A list of major international holidays is provided in Appendix 1 to illustrate how important it is to be aware of occurrences that could slow the research project or grind it to a halt altogether. The holidays cited are for countries where research is frequently conducted on a global basis and represent only national holidays. The following Web site can provide similar detailed information for other countries around the globe: *http://en.wikipedia.org/wiki/Category:Public_holidays_by_country.*

Another Web site that lists public holidays, time zones and languages spoken for countries worldwide is: *http://wrc.lingnet.org/areastd.htm.*

While it is crucial to avoid conflicts with public holidays, you should also treat religious and traditional holidays with extra care when preparing your research schedule. While public holidays may result in closed offices and few available participants for your research, holidays such as Valentine's Day (or cultural equivalents), election days,

Cinco de Mayo (Mexico), Halloween or St. Patrick's Day and the week between Christmas and New Year's Day (United States), and certain festivals in India may lead to similarly poor response rates or focus group participation.

Privacy laws are also more strictly regarded in certain countries. Germany, in particular, is a very good example of this. Focus group participants' or survey respondents' surnames remain confidential in the research vendors' files; they cannot be released to the end client.

When conducting business-to-business research, most German participants/respondents will typically be willing to describe the *type* of industry in which they work and possibly their own job responsibilities, but almost certainly they will avoid disclosing their companies' names as well as their official job titles. Even more difficult can be the process of scheduling on-site corporate interviews at participants' workplaces. German managers do not want nonemployees in the office environment where potentially confidential materials could be viewed or work could be disrupted in any way.

Levels of formality, meeting protocol and cultural behaviors all can have an effect on the success of your research, from your kick-off meeting with a foreign research supplier to an on-site depth interview in China. Use your lead supplier to clarify those cultural differences you might otherwise not be aware of. Some classic examples include the following:[2]

- Russia: Punctuality is often not as important to the Russians as it typically is in, for example, US meetings. Business meetings (and thus, by default, also focus groups) are likely to begin even an hour later than you see in the project schedule.

- Italy: Italian meetings can seem very unorganized as everyone will talk at the same time. Rules need to be established to help ensure that your agenda is followed.

- South Korea: Eye contact is not maintained throughout conversations here. If you try to do so, you are likely to be perceived as angry by your Korean colleagues.

- Brazil: Always address your contacts here by their title and surname rather than by their first name.

- China: Always carry business cards with you and accept cards from contacts with an attitude of respect.

In all Asian-Pacific countries, business cards are consistently presented upon introduction, often with formalities. Do not write on a business card presented to you and avoid putting it out of sight immediately (particularly in your back pocket, for gentlemen); this is considered extremely disrespectful.[3]

Even in countries you expect to be similar to your own, for instance for Americans conducting research with a

British supplier, there can be unexpected cultural variations. The British are not prone to emotional business encounters and expect an "appropriate" distance during conversations as well as limited eye contact and hand gestures.[4]

Above all, you must maintain a healthy respect for the cultures in the countries where you are conducting your research. After all, while you are bringing business to the regions, they are providing you with a necessary service. And you are a guest, a foreigner to them. If you exhibit this respect, however, the slight errors in protocol that can and do occur will be forgiven and your supplier team will willingly work with you to get the project done within the required schedule and to your expectations.

Chapter 6 Take-Aways

☑ Cultural issues that can affect research include such factors as:

- Different perspectives on numerical rating scales

- Attitudes toward schedules

- Interactions between focus group participants

- Gender

- Socioeconomic classes

- Holidays and major events/festivals

- Privacy laws

- Levels of formality and protocol in meetings

7

Crossing Language Barriers

Language issues can create formidable barriers for the international researcher—and international business people—for a variety of reasons. Consider the fact that there are numerous dialects and subdialects in China alone. There are 16 official languages in India. And keep in mind there are differences between and among American English, Canadian English, Australian English and British English that should be researched. Are you prepared to meet the required translation needs based on where your research might be conducted?

The most obvious problems in conducting research in other countries are the result of poor or incorrect translations from one language into another. Not all translation services (or research suppliers) can translate all languages with the same degree of accuracy. Always check the firms' references and credentials to identify the best qualified translators for your project based on the subject matter and countries the research project is expected to be conducted in.

There is endless potential for such errors due to any of the following issues:

- Technical terminology (terms, for example, specific to handheld computer products).

- Industry jargon: terms specific, for example, to business in general or even to a particular industry, such as the medical industry, that would be readily understood by physicians but not by a layperson.

- Idioms: terms readily understood in one language but not directly transferable by translation into another language.

- Variations in spellings from one dialect to another, which can alter meanings.

- Conversion from symbols, sounds and other alphabets to English alphabetic characters: When converting from one medium to another, much can be lost in translation.

Translation of Research Materials

Terms and phrases in research are an example of the difficulty in direct translation. In fact, translations may not just be confusing, but words can even take on an entirely different meaning when translated. The resulting mistranslation can result in poor research results due to the respondents' limited understanding of the questions and concepts you were originally attempting to convey.

These misunderstandings can frequently be alleviated to a great extent by insisting on a "back-translation" process. This involves a two-way translation where the initially translated version of your screener, questionnaire and/or discussion guide is then translated back into the original language. Once your questionnaire is translated, for example, from English to French, it is then translated *back* from the French version into English. This will help to ensure that idioms and technical or business terms are clearly translated before being used in the research. During this exercise, rough spots and errors in the initial translation become more readily apparent and can then be corrected before the project fieldwork begins so that you are certain that you are saying exactly what you were intending to say. If corrections are made, "back-translate" those changes as well.

The accuracy of the translation itself is not the only barrier caused by language differences between countries in a research study. The length of your questionnaire may vary substantially once it is translated. While this can be positive news if the length becomes shorter, unfortunately that is not what happens.

If your English questionnaire version requires 15 minutes of telephone interviewing time in the field, it might require 20 or more minutes of interviewing time to convey the same message in German. The essence of the questions is the same, but the wording takes the interviewer more time to express in German. The result is longer interviews, which then are likely to result in a higher cost per interview (CPI) in your German markets.

Similarly, translation issues can also affect the length of your international focus groups. If the wording of your discussion guide requires lengthier descriptions in, for example, Russian, there is little doubt that your focus groups will extend beyond the length of your domestic versions of the same groups.

I strongly recommend that you pre-test your questionnaire or discussion guide first in your native language and preferably in a domestic setting. You may want to revise it even before translating it. In any event, you must be prepared to make any necessary revisions in translation soon after the initial focus group or the first day of interviewing.

Interpretation in the Research Study

Just as important as accurate translation in an international research project is the need for *highly skilled* interpreters when moderating focus groups or conducting in-depth moderating qualitative interviews in another language. While English is recognized as a key language in the global business arena, you cannot assume that business people (and even less so the average consumer) will be able to converse at length in other than their native tongue.

Providing a native-speaking, qualified person to conduct groups and depth interviews helps to put respondents much more at ease and helps to ensure that they fully understand what questions are being asked of them and the use of local idioms and industry or technological terms will be correctly translated. It is important that the interpreters have experience with research as well as the necessary language skills for the industry for which you are conducting the research. They need to understand the importance of avoiding leading questions, how to keep discussions on track with the research objectives and so on.

Some research vendors may have such qualified interpreters or bilingual focus group moderators/interviewers on their own internal staff, but frequently they will find it necessary to subcontract this service using interpreters who have worked with them in the past and proven to be particularly skilled in specific languages. While this is an acceptable practice, if you are in any way concerned about the interpreters who are selected to work on your project, discuss this with your contracted vendor and ask for references and details regarding the interpreters' professional experience.

If you are addressing business audiences in your research, specifically request that moderators and/or interviewers have had sufficient experience with business-to-business research studies. By the very nature of their hectic schedules, business people are more expensive to recruit and much more difficult to coordinate research interviews with. The higher their position and the larger their companies are, the greater the value they place on their own time. They expect interviewers and moderators to be professional and to treat them with respect. A novice interviewer who is checking the clock and perhaps being a bit flippant is not acceptable in any language.

Furthermore, the coordination of international focus groups and in-depth interviews conducted in research facilities frequently requires the inclusion of an *additional* interpreter. Unless you and your research team are fluent in the language that the discussion or interviews are conducted in, it is common practice to have an interpreter in the back viewing room. And it is every bit as important to brief the interpreter as it is to brief the focus group moderator.

The interpreter needs to thoroughly understand the objectives of the research study as well as the terminology that will be used in the discussions. To ensure this is the case, the interpreters should always be briefed prior to the groups along with the focus group moderator. During this briefing you should always be sure to clarify any technical terms, industry jargon and product or service names which might not otherwise directly translate into the language the groups will be conducted in. This will prevent any possible misinterpretation in the analysis of the results as well as the potentially resulting confusion among the decision-makers viewing the groups or the resulting translated versions of the videotapes. Likewise, the interpreters are frequently included in the debriefing following each set of focus groups for precisely the same reasons.

This interpreter will provide "simultaneous" interpretation for the viewers. For example, for an American team viewing focus groups in France, the interpreter would repeat in English precisely what has just been said by participants in the group in French. Generally he or she will indicate either by name, by physical description or by seating position which participant has made which comments. Some interpreters will even go one step further and attempt to creatively incorporate "different" voices for each person speaking. It is this interpreted version of the sessions that is usually dubbed over the group or interview videotapes to allow viewing by the clients in their native language.

The interpreter is often seated in the viewing room and generally will wear headphones to hear the precise dialogue occurring in the group. Occasionally, facilities will provide a separate booth for the interpreter outside of the viewing room. This allows to the interpreter to concentrate without any possible background distractions from the viewers while the interpreted version of the discussion is broadcast over the speakers into the viewing room.

While we have been concentrating on translation and interpretation issues, another important concern to address is the communication with your international research vendors. While typically your primary vendor contact will be able to speak your language to some degree, be careful to confirm that all of your requests, inputs and queries are *completely* understood. If often helps to speak more slowly than usual when conversing with someone whose English is not his or her first or even second language. Also, do not rely solely on brief telephone conversations that can be easily misinterpreted.

Instead, follow up on your client/vendor discussions and meetings with detailed email messages that simply and clearly summarize what was covered in your initial messages and conversation. At the very first indication that a miscommunication may have occurred with your vendor, you should act quickly to clarify your expectations or the vendor's intentions.

Chapter 7 Take-Aways

☑ Language can create barriers in international research in terms of:

- Technical terminology
- Industry jargon
- Idioms
- Variations in spellings
- Conversion from symbols, sounds and other alphabets to English alphabetic characters

☑ Avoid language barriers by:

- "Back-translation" process
- Pre-testing screeners, questionnaires and discussion guides
- Requesting native-speaking, qualified interpreters and moderators
- Arranging for simultaneous interpretation during focus groups
- Thoroughly briefing the supplier team, moderators and interpreters
- Putting all communications in writing

8

On Your Mark . . . Get Set . . .

The "kick-off" meeting is the first official meeting you and your team will have with your selected vendor before the project begins. Think of your project kick-off meeting as your last chance to get everything organized in just the right way for your study before it launches. There are always means of correcting any problems throughout the project, but this is your final opportunity to avoid the pitfalls from the very beginning. Don't go anywhere in the world without it!

145

Depending on the location of your selected research supplier, the kick-off meeting may be conducted in person or via teleconference or videoconference. Any of these formats will allow a detailed question and answer session regarding the project budget, timeline, specifications, and other matters. Still, if at all possible, a face-to-face meeting with the key contact(s) from the supplier side can be very helpful in establishing a more personal connection and a "buy-in" to the research study.

The kick-off meeting generally occurs within a few days to a week from when you actually award the project to your selected supplier. The best use of this session is to confirm that everyone involved in the study is "on the same page" in terms of the research project plans as well as the client's expectations. Be certain to provide all participants with a detailed agenda for this meeting, although frequently the research vendor will coordinate this task for you. Your RFP and the proposal you selected should be used to develop a checklist such as in Exhibit 8.1, to be certain that you cover all the key concerns related to your project.

You can, of course, add more details but generally this meeting is a starting point so you are establishing the details rather than presenting them to the team.

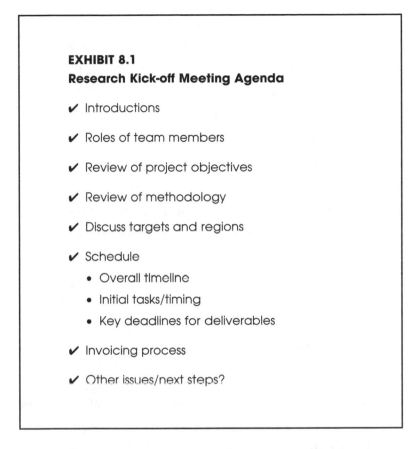

EXHIBIT 8.1
Research Kick-off Meeting Agenda

✔ Introductions

✔ Roles of team members

✔ Review of project objectives

✔ Review of methodology

✔ Discuss targets and regions

✔ Schedule
  • Overall timeline
  • Initial tasks/timing
  • Key deadlines for deliverables

✔ Invoicing process

✔ Other issues/next steps?

Introductions

Who is participating in the kick-off meeting? Is everyone there who should be? Is everyone present going to be an active member of the project team for this research, either on the client side or on the supplier side?

Bear in mind that it is not uncommon to have, for example, product managers/engineers, advertising account executives and other managers closely tied to the research objectives involved in the kick-off meeting. This helps to provide a well-rounded picture of the need for the research and how they each anticipate being able to utilize the end results. This does not necessarily mean that these participants will play an active role throughout the course of the research—or even in this initial meeting.

For those who are identified as permanent members of the project team, now is a good time to confirm who the key contact in charge is for the client and who will represent the vendor. If this is not immediately established, project tasks can become confusing as no one is certain precisely who has the final decision-making authority at the other end.

Establish Roles

What specifically is the client responsible for, and what is the vendor expected to be responsible for in terms of management, updates, sign-offs on questionnaires, scripts, briefing of interviewers, monitoring of initial interviews, reports, and so forth?

Typically, these roles have previously been spelled out in detail both by the client in the RFP and the vendor in the proposal. Formal clarification of these expectations, however, should be confirmed during the kick-off meeting. Some common divisions of tasks and responsibilities between the market research supplier and the research client are indicated in Exhibit 8.2.

While it is acceptable to have a number of people on

EXHIBIT 8.2
Supplier and Client Responsibilities

Research Supplier	*Research Client*
Design screener, discussion guides, questionnaire	Inputs to and approval of screener, discussion guides, questionnaire
Obtaining sample/devising sampling plan to meet quota requirements	Providing portions of sample as applicable (i.e, customer lists)
Project briefing with managers, moderators, interviewers	Participation in and inputs into project briefing
Pre-testing survey	Monitor initial interviews, provide feedback
Conduct focus groups	Participate actively in focus group debriefing with moderator
Provide ongoing reports re: project status	Respond to vendor re: specific concerns re: project
Prepare report/ presentation of results	Provide inputs to report and presentation before distribution to internal corporate clients

teams on both the vendor and client sides present at the meeting, it is strongly recommended that you have only one key contact on both sides to keep the meeting running smoothly, with perhaps one alternate on each side for backup responses. Too many people responding back and forth can allow for decisions being made that not everyone is aware of, potentially leading to errors and confusion.

Review of Project Objectives

Certainly by the time the kick-off meeting occurs, you and the account executive or project manager from your selected vendor have discussed your research objectives in what may seem like exhausting detail. This session, however, is your last re-visit of what you want to accomplish before the actual launch. You will need to ensure that all of the parties involved with the study clearly understand these objectives in exactly the same way.

Review each of the key objectives from your RFP in terms of your information requirements and your expectations based on the research supplier's final version of the proposal. Does everyone agree that the objectives are going to be met according to their expectations? Be certain to clarify all of the details and idiosyncrasies so that everyone is working toward identical goals. Ask questions and encourage all of the meeting participants to do so as well.

Review of the Proposed Methodology

By the time this meeting takes place, you will have already selected the vendor's proposal, thereby indicating that you agree entirely with the methodology described in the document. The kick-off meeting is, however, an excellent opportunity to fine-tune the methodology, perhaps identifying even better ways to obtain the sample, reach target audiences and gather data. Such additional brainstorming should be encouraged at this session, by all means. It is highly unlikely that the whole proposal will be rewritten, but clarifications that are discussed in the meeting often lead to improvements.

You also should remember that any changes to the proposal as it was initially presented to you can (and most likely will) result in changes to the proposed budget as well. The estimate in the supplier's proposal is based on the methodology and specifications as they initially detailed it, not as it is refined in future conversations.

Confirm Targets and Scope

While you should have already stated who you expected to conduct the research with and where you expect the research to be conducted, your selected vendor may have made various other suggestions along these lines in their proposal. What attributes will determine if a contact is qualified to participate in your research study? Now is the time to make the final decision regarding whom you want to talk to and where they are to be found, not just in terms of countries, but in terms of industries, business versus consumers, customers versus noncustomers, brand preferences and so on.

Timeline

By the time the kick-off meeting occurs, you as the client will have outlined in the RFP all of your own expectations regarding the research schedule and who is to deliver what and when. Likewise, your selected research supplier has provided you with a detailed proposed timeline for each phase and task involved in the study for your review and approval.

This initial project meeting is the time to fine-tune and, if needed, finalize the project calendar. While both you and your vendor realize what expectations there are concerning the schedule, you should be certain to ask questions about where slowdowns are more likely to occur and how these can possibly be avoided or at least limited.

Any information you have promised to provide prior to the design phase of the research project, if provided in a timely manner, will help to get things moving right on schedule early in the process. Any delays on the part of either party are likely to delay the study, so both the client and the research supplier need to meet their dead-lines or notify all pertinent team members of any problems and the resulting schedule changes in order to keep potential project delays to an absolute minimum.

Payment

Typically, research vendors will state their payment expectations in their proposals. The kick-off meeting, however, provides an opportunity to discuss any changes to their invoicing schedule you might like to see. If your supplier, for example, has requested a payment of 50% upon project initiation and 50% upon delivery of the final research report, you might have internal policies in place that require a different breakdown for payment of professional services. During the meeting, if you have not received earlier agreement on this, you might request payment terms of 25% initially, 25% once fielding has begun, and 50% upon the completion of the study.

It is also important to clarify who will be coordinating the invoicing process on your project. Who will you call with questions related to project invoices? Where are payments to be sent? While often this information is very clear on the invoices, it is helpful to have it on file from the beginning.

Next Steps

What comes next and when? Determine when the team (or appropriate members of the team) will next meet to discuss the project status. While you have everyone together, preferably with their calendars in hand, try to schedule the next meeting and its agenda to ensure that you can get on everyone's calendar before other meetings push your schedule back.

Ask questions, to be sure everything is covered and everyone understands the answers, even if they may have been mentioned before. This is the best time for clarification. For a multinational study, it will be particularly important to clarify any difference in methodology, expectations, etc., in *each* of the regions you are including in your study.

Let's look at a more specific example of a kick-off meeting. Example 8.1 is a condensed version of an RFP that will serve as the basis for the kick-off meeting.

Example 8.1

**PROPOSAL FOR PDA MARKETING RESEARCH
(condensed)
PREPARED FOR: PERSONAL COMPUTER INC.**

1. Introduction and Research Objectives

Personal Computer Inc. (PCI) requires research to gain a better understanding of their executive consumers as well as an understanding of the purchase decision process and the role of price in the decision to purchase PDAs. This research is to be conducted in the United States and in Germany.

The key objective of this study is to gather more information and better understand how the product category (vs. other wireless devices), pricing, marketing strategy, etc., influence and effect the purchase decision of a PDA.

2. Targets and Methodology

Of primary interest in this study are consumers who plan to purchase a PDA in the next 6 months who meet the following specifications:

- Are in the 25–50 age groups.
- Own their own business/are self-employed or are employed in companies with 500 or fewer employees (a mix of company sizes).
- Work away from their main office at least 25% of the time.
- Plan to purchase a PDA within the next 6 months (any brand).
- Plan to use the PDA primarily for business purposes.
- Make the product choice themselves or have significant input into the product choice.

The study will be conducted as a Web survey using a choice-based conjoint exercise to model the PDA purchase decision. Price sensitivity will be measured as well.

Sample will be obtained through WebAnalysis Corporation's online research panels in the US and Germany. There will be 250 completed surveys in each country.

3. Deliverables

All reports and tables will be provided in electronic format unless hard copies are requested. The following are included in the cost estimate:

- Management presentation (videoconference format).
- Final report.
- Simulation model for internal use of the choice-based conjoint data.
- All data tables from the survey.

4. Timetable

Approximately 40 business days will be required to design, coordinate, conduct and provide the final data related to the project as it is defined in the preceding sections.

5. Proposed Estimate

The cost of conducting the proposed research project is $70,000. Changes to the proposed respondent qualifications, sample source, sample sizes, etc., will result in cost revisions.

EXHIBIT 8.3
PDA Marketing Research
"Kick-Off" Meeting Agenda

✔ Introductions

- Client team/roles

- Supplier team/roles

✔ Review of Project Objectives

- Gather information/better understand the PDA product category, pricing and market strategy influence/affect in the purchase decision for a PDA

✔ Project Specifications

- Methodology: Web survey with choice-based conjoint exercise

- Regions: United States and Germany (250 completes/country)

- Targets:

    —Are in the 25–50 age groups

    —Own their own business/are self-employed or are employed in companies with 500 or fewer employees (a mix of company sizes)

EXHIBIT 8.3 (Continued)

—Work away from their main office at least 25% of the time.

—Plan to purchase a PDA within the next 6 months (any brand)

—Plan to use the PDA primarily for business purposes

— Make the product choice themselves or have significant input into the product choice

- Sample Source: online panel

✔ Schedule

- Project will take about 40 business days from start to completion

- Need to set deadlines—when does client need final data latest?/discuss timeline by task

✔ Invoicing Process

- Discuss billing procedures with client— what % billed at what point?

- Purchase order requirements?

✔ Other Comments/Next Steps

Let us now assume that the client has contracted with the research vendor based on the preceding proposal. The contract is signed and now it is time for the kick-off meeting for the project. The agenda in Exhibit 8.3 provides a good outline for this meeting based on the proposal example.

Chapter 8 Take-Aways

☑ Hold a kick-off meeting with the supplier before the research begins.

☑ The kick-off meeting agenda should include:
- Introductions
- The roles of the team members
- Clarification of the research objectives
- Review of the proposed methodology
- Confirmation of targets and scope
- Establishment of client/vendor roles
- The timeline
- The invoicing process
- Covering next steps

9

Coordinating the International Research Project

There is no special formula to ensure that you will manage your international research project so that all of the results come in on time and without error. The key has less to do with your personal management efforts during the course project and is related more to the initial homework that you conduct. If you check references, look at the details and select the correct vendor, your actual management time will be related more to reviewing data and making decisions rather than overseeing the efforts of the vendor.

Your Overall Role

In your RFP (see Chapter 1), you specified what your expectations were of the research supplier and what responsibilities you expected to take during the course of your research project. That information should also have been discussed and clarified during the initial research project kick-off meeting (see Chapter 8). There are some additional considerations, however.

Your Role in Designing the Research Tools

If you have a strong marketing research background, you may consider drafting the initial questionnaire and/or the focus group discussion guides yourself. Yet you should think about the "pros" and "cons" to taking on this task before you actually do so.

On the positive side, there is likely to be a notable cost savings as a result of your doing the work, assuming that you have done a fairly good job at designing these research tools. You will have cut the total number of professional hours that your supplier would have had to devote to the research design phase. In addition, who better would understand the necessary questions to ask as well as the appropriate wording of these questions?

In the negative column, however, as an internal manager close to the project, you might inadvertently infuse some degree of bias into your questionnaire or the moderator's discussion guides. Furthermore, while you may have some degree of experience with questionnaire design, if you are not entirely familiar with the vendor's proposed methodology, any work which you complete may have to be rewritten or redesigned in part by the supplier to allow the appropriate analysis to be conducted.

I strongly suggest that, even if you do have a strong research background, you should step back and allow the vendor to design the questionnaire and/or discussion guides. Define your role as providing the necessary inputs for the first draft of the materials and later critiquing the proposed materials and as having the final approval of the materials. In this way, the vendor will benefit from your expertise in research and knowledge of the research subject matter and the internal issues related to it. In turn, you are able to maintain the final approval and sign-off authority before the research study is fielded.

Vendor Staff

It may help you to have an idea of the "players" on the market research supplier side so you are aware of who is

EXHIBIT 9.1
Vendor Staff in Research Projects

✔ Account Executive is likely to be the contact who sold you the project and often is the regular contact related to the progress of your study. May be involved in reporting and the presentation in conjunction with the Project Manager.

✔ Project Manager is involved with the day-to-day status of your project and involved in the management of the rest of the staff working on the study. Likely to be writing the final report and be involved in the final presentation of the results.

✔ Research Analyst/Statistician is typically responsible for the "number-crunching" and providing the graphs and statistical analysis involved in the reporting of your research data.

✔ Interviewer Supervisors are the very necessary but often under-appreciated staff members responsible for the quality control on survey interviews and focus group recruiting. They manage the interviewing staff and are typically responsible for the interview validation process.

✔ Research Interviewers conduct the research interviews and/or recruit focus group/in-person respondents.

✔ Focus Group Moderator leads focus group discussions and typically conducts debriefings with the client viewers following each group.

✔ Data Processing people are responsible for the quality of the data and typically also program CATI questionnaires for surveys; they also run data tables with cross-tabulations and provide information necessary for the analysts/statisticians.

typically doing what aspect of your study. Exhibit 9.1 provides an overview of who is likely to be involved with your project from start to finish in the vendor's offices.

Changes During the Project

While it is not unusual for changes to occur when the research project is finally in the field, it is important that both parties agree to any changes in writing to prevent any misunderstandings. Emails typically will suffice for this, although if there is a formal contract, as is often the case with large-scale global studies, a formal letter, memo or even an addendum to the contract may be required and is certainly recommended.

Briefing the Study

It is extremely important to include the moderator, your research supplier's project manager and any interpreters in the pre-focus group briefing at each location you travel to for your project. If they do not clearly understand all the terminology and nuances of your research topic, they will not be able to properly convey the necessary questions, descriptions and demonstrations to the participants.

Seriously consider using an "active briefing" process. This is accomplished by having the local research supplier team members repeat back to you in their own words what they understand their tasks to be, specifically and in detail. This will help to readily identify any potential areas of misunderstanding from the beginning. Also be certain to allow adequate time for your briefing prior to beginning the initial session or interview in each location in order to avoid any unnecessary confusion.

Participation in the Process

It is not unusual for the key client contact to take a more active role than other team members during the research study. In addition to providing inputs related to the research tools (questionnaire, screeners, discussion guides, etc.), you may also want to monitor the initial interviews or recruiting calls in order to get a feel for both how the interviewers are performing as well as how well respondents are comprehending the questions which are being asked. Are there any wording issues or concepts that are not thoroughly clear to them? This is a valuable exercise and can generally be conducted remotely from your office or home rather than having to be on site at the vendor's facility.

The checklist in Exhibit 9.2 provides a general list of potential management tasks in which you, as the client, may wish to be involved. The more active the role you choose to play, the better you will be acquainted with your research study and its results.

EXHIBIT 9.2
Research Client Management Tasks

✔ Participate in the kick-off meeting.

✔ Provide inputs to the screeners, questionnaire and/or discussion guides.

✔ Proof and approve final screeners, questionnaire and/or discussion guides.

✔ Participate in the interviewer/moderator briefings.

✔ Review "back-translations" of all research project materials.

✔ Monitor interviews/recruitment calls.

✔ Provide inputs to any potential screener, questionnaire or discussion guide revisions.

✔ Attend focus groups and the related debriefings.

✔ Provide inputs re: cross-tabulations for data processing.

✔ Review draft of final report and provide inputs.

Chapter 9 Take-Aways

☑ In managing an international research project:

- Be sure that vendor/client roles are clearly defined.

- Determine client role in the design process.

- Avoid any bias that would cause the data to be misrepresentative.

- A number of the research vendor's staff may be involved in your study, including:

  —Account Executive

  —Project Manager

  —Research Analyst/Statistician

  —Interviewer Supervisors

  —Research Interviewers

  —Focus Group Moderator

  —Data Processing

☑ Briefing the study is important:

- Include supplier project manager, moderator, interpreters as applicable.

- Utilize an "active briefing" process.

☑ Participation in the research process:

- Consider active role on the client side
- Provide inputs re: design
- Monitor interviews
- Final report approval/inputs

10

Unusual Suspects

Problems with Your Project

No project is without its mishaps, but how you handle these mishaps when they occur could actually be the determining factor in the success or failure of your research project. Addressing the problems directly with your supplier is an obvious first step, but it helps to have some suggestions of your own as to what you expect them to do to make amends and get the project back on track.

Here are some examples of how to deal with a few of the different problems that can (and occasionally have) come up during international research studies.

Problems Filling Quotas

The research supplier is having extreme difficulties in filling the quota groups for your study because the incidence of the targeted respondents is much lower than initially anticipated.

Consider the possible causes of this problem. Was the estimated incidence which you initially supplied or that the research vendor recommended for the various quota groups incorrect? Are the difficulties potentially due to a methodology issue or could the sample lists be incorrect or incomplete? Determining the potential cause(s) of the problem should help you to figure out a solution to the problem.

Unreliable Sample Source

The proposed sample source has proven unreliable, thus stalling progress on your study.

Who suggested the sample source and/or obtained the sample being used in the study? Was the incorrect sample purchased through an error at your end, at the vendor's end, or was it misrepresented by the list broker? There may be some cause for discounted sample costs, but meanwhile you will need to address the more immediate problem and identify another list source.

Consider the potential reasons why the sample is not working well for your project:

- A large percentage of the contacts on the sample list are no longer at the phone numbers provided.

  Purchased lists may often contain older and less reliable contact information, if the list supplier has not provided regular updates to the sample to "weed out" outdated information. If the supplier's sample is not regularly updated (i.e., every 6 months), you should identify a list through a different list broker who does maintain current records.

- The contacts on the list are current. However, they are not qualified for the research study.

  A list of names for a research study is only as helpful as the number of qualified respondents/ participants it produces. Check to see if the list broker has more details available per contact. For instance, if your existing list currently includes only contact names and telephone numbers for people over 30 years of age in a given region, perhaps more details are available to "pre-qualify" your list. Determine if you can obtain a list of contacts who are 30 years old and over or who are plus or minus 3 years, for example, who fit the profile you are looking for in your survey screening questions.

The list supplier may be able to provide a list using additional qualifiers such as household income levels, professions, educational backgrounds, etc. While it is still advisable to re-screen contacts during the interview process, you may find that you are more successful obtaining qualified respondents this way.

- All attempts at buying a list have not generated the necessary sample for the study. Now what?

Consider using the services of a panel research firm in order to obtain the sample necessary for your study. There are a number of highly-regarded research companies which specialize specifically in developing and maintaining research panels. While typically the firm will control the sample and send out the invitation to selected panelists to participate in your study, pulling contacts from a panel has the attractive benefit of knowing who will be qualified in advance for at least a good number of your screening questions. This sample source may help "jump-start" your otherwise stalled study.

Translation Errors

Your survey is in the field, and it appears that your vendor has made some significant errors in the translation of your questionnaire.

First, you should determine if the errors that have been made are immediately correctable. Were the errors grammatical or were they actually more technical in nature?

Grammatical misinterpretations, while inconvenient and even perhaps a bit embarrassing from a professional standpoint, are not as likely to cause any real problems with your data. Generally, the necessary corrections can be made once they are discovered without presenting any major concerns or requiring callbacks to survey respondents.

Of greater concern, however, are those errors that either have provided an incorrect description of your company's product or service concept, or which give a poor or totally mistaken interpretation of key questions related to your research objectives. What effect will these errors have on your research's end data? For example, how many of the completed interviews were conducted using the incorrect version of the questionnaire?

If the errors are only grammatical in nature and *another* translator has confirmed that the intended meaning still should be clear to the respondents, you should be able to include the previously completed questionnaires in your final data. If, however, the translation errors have misrepresented your questions, products, concepts, etc., the responses collected to date may not be a true reflection of the respondents' opinions.

Take steps to make the corrections as quickly as possible and preferably using a different translator altogether. Once again, you should arrange to conduct a "back-translation" to double check for any other potential errors. The corrected version of the questionnaire should be used for all remaining interviews. For those interviews already completed using the initial questionnaire, you should make sure that your research supplier arranges follow-up calls with the respondents to ask the necessary questions to provide the correct data for the survey. If any of the initial respondents cannot be re-contacted, the interviews should be entirely replaced at the vendor's cost.

Ineffective Methodology

Your study is underway, but it has become obvious that the methodology is not working.

First, without casting blame, you should focus on the key issue, which, depending on the timing required for results, is to get the study back on track. What can be used from the study thus far? The sample, the questionnaire, another element?

Also, what can be done to correct the methodology itself? For example, can you change from a telephone survey to an online survey? Should the research have been conducted with an initial qualitative phase instead of rushing right into a quantitative study?

Provided that the overall questionnaire remains the same, you should be able to conduct the study in different ways in different regions to complete the study in a timely manner. For example, if you expected to conduct all of the interviews as telephone surveys, you may find that you need to switch gears and conduct all the interviews in China in person instead. Or instead of a Web survey across all regions, a mail survey or telephone interview may need to be incorporated in different regions. Always bear in mind that there are differences around the world in what will and what will not work in terms of gathering research data. It is often necessary to be flexible and adjust the study accordingly, sometimes even after the project has begun.

Once ways to correct the immediate problem have been finalized, then you should discuss how the problem occurred in the first place. Was it your own internal team or was it the research supplier who recommended the research component that is not meeting expectations? If it was requested and/or approved by the client team, did the vendor suggest another, potentially preferable substitution? In either of these cases, you should not be quick to penalize the vendor in terms of project expenses. If the vendor made the recommendation, the vendor possibly should be responsible for all costs related to any changes. Who absorbs the cost should be determined before proceeding.

Problems with Prototypes

Your prototypes, which you had planned to use in the research, have been delayed by customs officials.

There are various potential solutions to this particular problem depending on the expected delay:

- Is the delay an immediate one only? For example, a colleague was carrying the prototypes as baggage and is held up by long lines at the airport to complete some unexpected forms. This may only delay the first evening of focus groups. It may be possible to push the groups to a slightly later time on the first evening by offering slightly higher cooperation fees to participants for the inconvenience. If the delay is going to stretch a bit longer, then one or both of your groups that evening may need to be cancelled unless alternative means of presenting the concepts are available.

- If you shipped the prototypes prior to the groups and you know that they are awaiting approval from the customs officials, all that may be required is answering a few questions and potentially paying a fee greater than initially anticipated. Often this can be handled by the supplier prior to the meeting of the initial groups and the problem can be averted.

- Finally, if it becomes clear that there is no way

you will be able to retrieve your prototypes prior to this particular set of groups you need to weigh your options depending on what you can do without them. If you can use any other visual, such as sketches of the designs (of course you have taken them along as backup!) for the initial groups without drastically impacting participants' understanding, you can try to conduct the groups in this way. If the groups are entirely dependent on the prototype presentation, it would be advisable to reschedule the groups when they are available, moving on with the other countries on the itinerary and getting back to the delayed group at another time, if feasible.

Regardless of the situation and the resulting solution, it is imperative that you take steps to avoid the same issue for the remaining groups. Shipping and confirming receipt of the prototypes with your supplier well in advance of the scheduled groups can help prevent this problem from occurring.

Insufficient Number of Participants

You planned to use three focus groups. Too few participants arrive to participate in each of the three focus groups you are conducting.

Even a small group is better than no group, at least to

begin with! Given that you probably cannot move up the schedule for any of your other groups or travel anyway, you should allow the "mini" groups to continue and glean what information you can at this point.

You should, however, discuss the causes of the poor attendance with your supplier. If the recruiting was not conducted early enough, follow-up calls or invitations were neglected or delayed, or due to any other otherwise correctable issue, you may want to request that the groups be repeated at the vendor's expense (or at least at an agreed-upon decreased cost). While it may not be feasible for you or your team members to view the additional groups, you will be able to view the tapes of the groups once they are completed.

Unclear Discussions

The focus groups appear to be going well, but those of you watching in the viewing room are not sure what is being said.

At the very least, this is a very annoying situation! You should conduct a meeting between group sessions with the moderator at the facility as well as with your supplier/ project manager to discuss the problem. It simply may be that a refresher briefing is necessary, or you may actually need to arrange for a different interpreter for the next evening's groups.

As long as the moderator has grasped the concept, the

interpretation in the viewing room is more of an inconvenience than a major problem. Translated transcripts of the groups can be provided so you should be able to get all of the input you require from the groups.

And, naturally, in addition to the preceding examples, there are always the unexpected "little" surprise situations that occur. These can throw panic into even the most stalwart researcher, but ultimately they can be overcome as some of these examples indicate in Appendix 5, "Tales from the Trenches: Anecdotes from International Researchers."

Chapter 10 Take-Aways

☑ Problems can and often do occur during international research projects:

- Address problems directly with your supplier

- Offer suggestions of your own that will meet your requirements

☑ Be prepared for the types of problems that can occur such as:

- Poor quality sample

- Incorrect translations

- Wrong methodologies selected for some regions

- Prototypes for testing delayed in customs

- Low focus group attendance

- Simultaneous interpretation is not accurate/understandable

11

Reporting

"Who, What, When, Where, Why, How"

The format of your research report as well as the style and medium of the resulting presentations are likely to vary depending on the audience you anticipate for them.

Ask yourself first who will see the final results of your study? The informational needs of your audience will vary significantly, depending on who is reviewing the results. Consider for a moment how each of the following groups would look at your results:

- C-Level/executive/senior corporate managers
- International group managers
- Advertising agency representatives
- Sales staff (domestic and/or global)
- Engineering/product development managers/team members
- Marketing managers
- Research team members

What will each of these different audiences need to learn from the research data? The needs and objectives are likely to vary greatly by audience, and if there are multiple audiences, you will need to hit on the key points for each group.

You need to look at the following considerations for each audience to be addressed:

- Where will the presentation be conducted?
- When will they need top-line results versus a final analysis and report?
- Should you opt for an in-person presentation versus a conference call or just a final delivery of the report less all of the "bells and whistles?"

- How will management actually use the results of the study?

Location

Where will the presentation be conducted?

The higher the level of your audience, the better it is to get the data in front of them. If an in-person presentation is possible, do it! Furthermore, the executive level "buy-in" to the research is increased by having the research supplier conduct or at least participate in a formal presentation of the study results.

Delivery Dates

When will they need top-line results versus a final analysis and report?

The higher the level, the more strategic the use of the research is likely to be. Keep key points bulleted and graphically presented to get the most important results presented in a minimum amount of time. Top-line summaries are more likely to get reviewed than lengthy reports with multiple addendums and data tables.

Example 11.1 is a sample of a top-line research report.[1] It is very concise and to the point. In this instance, the top-line report is based on a series of multinational focus groups. Note that quotations as well as research recommendations are not typically included in this initial report. This simply provides key general findings so that the client has some feel for what is going to come out of the research while the more detailed analysis is in progress. The top-line report may pull out well-documented findings by region if they are immediately apparent or their discussion can be delayed until the final analysis is completed.

Example 11.1
CENTRAL CELLULAR CORP.
SMALL BUSINESS CELLULAR USAGE STUDY

TOP-LINE RESULTS

1. INTRODUCTION

This top-line research report is based on a series of US and European focus groups for the Central Cellular Corporation (CCC). This is a brief summary of findings based on an initial review of the focus group results and will be supplemented with a full analysis of the results at the final presentation.

2. OBJECTIVES

The key objective for this study is to identify what cellular service purchasers and users in small businesses (between two and one hundred employees) look for in their service. Results will be used to fine-tune CCC's existing service offerings and identify advertising themes which will attract this business segment.

3. METHODOLOGY

A series of 16 focus groups were conducted in the US and Europe consisting of the following categories:

- San Francisco: 4 Groups
- New York: 4 groups

- London: 4 groups
- Frankfurt: 4 groups

Two groups in each city consisted of small business cellular service purchase decision-makers (i.e., purchasing managers, IT managers, CEOs, etc.), while the remaining two groups in each city consisted of employees within small businesses who use their own (not provided by their company) cellular phones/service primarily for business purposes.

In all groups, there were participants from a variety of different cellular providers' service plans.

4. TOP-LINE FINDINGS

Purchase Decision-Makers

- Cell phone service is a necessity in most small businesses, particularly:
  —in sales-related firms.
  —in companies where business travel is frequently required.
  —in companies centrally-located in the large cities where employees are commuting long distances to work.
- As necessary as cellular service is, it is also a "necessary evil" in that budget control is difficult to maintain and the review of the related billings is often confusing.
- They need to be able to better tailor their company's cellular service to meet their own specific needs:
  —Text messaging is seldom being used.
  —Voicemail options need to be enhanced.
  —Need a way to identify, by code or otherwise, calls related to various customers' projects, personal calls, etc.

Business End-Users

- While they are using their cell phones frequently, there is a preference among many users to use email when away from the office whenever possible because it does not allow as much room for misinterpretation. In addition, email provides documentation. This *is not the case* among sales representatives who prefer voicemail as it is more personal and more likely to prompt a response.

- In many cases, users have two cell phones to avoid issues related to reimbursement on their business cellular service bills.
- There is a good deal of frustration among users related to "dropped calls," either when they are "out of range" or going through a tunnel. As might be expected, this is particularly an issue for commuters on trains and subways.

Type of Presentation

How the presentation is conducted is generally based on an internal preference. The basic choices regarding the presentation are an in-person presentation versus a conference call versus a final delivery of the report without all of the "bells and whistles"?

While a formal presentation is recommended for high-level managers, a conference call "debriefing" and discussion (more of a Q&A session) could suffice for the research and/or marketing team. The choice is likely to depend on the relative strategic importance of the research that has been conducted.

Use(s) of the Study

How will management actually use the results of the study?

Any given research project may provide information for more than one group (i.e., marketing, customer service, human resources, product engineering, etc.) It is important to recognize the overall value of the research at two levels.

First, you should identify at the very beginning of the

RFP process what divisions/departments are likely to benefit most from the study as it is expected to be conducted. Without trying to recreate the research project to be "all things to all people," seek appropriate inputs for the research specifications.

Second, be open to recognizing where results unexpectedly yield useful information to areas of the business not previously foreseen when the project originated.

These are all viable issues that you should address in the early stages of your international research project. If you are aware of who your audience(s) will be at the outset of the study, you can ensure that the right questions are asked to get the answers that will be needed for decision-making. While no one project can ultimately be the answer to every marketing question, advance preparation can ensure the most usable results possible.

The final report is the culmination of the entire research project. If all has gone according to plan, the report should provide answers that allow you and your team to address your original research objectives. The answers might not always be the ones management would prefer to hear, but they will be useful to them as they deliberate before making decisions.

The format for the final report can vary, depending on your market research supplier's preferred format, your internal reporting requirements, and so on. One firm may provide the entire report as a slide presentation with notations, while another may have a more standard-looking bound document with detailed write-ups and quotes.

A final research report for your study, regardless of the countries the research encompassed or whether the study is qualitative or quantitative in nature, should include at least the information contained in Exhibit 11.1.

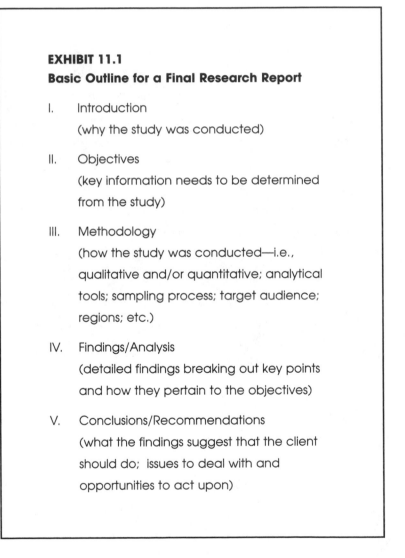

EXHIBIT 11.1
Basic Outline for a Final Research Report

I. Introduction
(why the study was conducted)

II. Objectives
(key information needs to be determined from the study)

III. Methodology
(how the study was conducted—i.e., qualitative and/or quantitative; analytical tools; sampling process; target audience; regions; etc.)

IV. Findings/Analysis
(detailed findings breaking out key points and how they pertain to the objectives)

V. Conclusions/Recommendations
(what the findings suggest that the client should do; issues to deal with and opportunities to act upon)

In addition to the points noted in Exhibit 11.1, generally the client will also be provided with any and all data tables, statistical analyses, transcripts of interviews or discussions, and/or videotapes of focus group sessions (translated, as applicable).

Chapter 11 Take-Aways

- ☑ The informational needs of your audience will vary based on who is reading the report or attending the research presentation.

- ☑ For each different audience consider:
  - Will there be a formal presentation and where will it be conducted?
  - When will they need top-line results versus the final analysis and report?
  - Presentation format—in-person, conference call or video conference?
  - How will they use the results of the study?

- ☑ The final research report may vary in format, but should include:
  - Introduction
  - Objectives
  - Methodology
  - Findings/Analysis
  - Conclusions/Recommendations

12

Ethics in International Research

Ethics obviously are a crucial element in all areas of the business world. However, they take on particular nuances when you are conducting an international project. You must be particularly conscientious and respectful of how other cultures would consider your research subject matter in particular and your methodologies in general. It is not just the legal aspects (such as the German privacy laws, which were mentioned earlier), but also the human aspects of research that come to the forefront when one is doing a study abroad.

A number of organizations offer ethical guidelines or codes for firms conducting marketing research in general and thus international research as well. These organizations include Council of American Survey Research Organizations (CASRO), the Market Research Association (MRA), and the European Society for Opinion and Marketing Research (ESOMAR).

ESOMAR's code is specifically targeted to companies conducting international research. The ethical guidelines of the other organizations, however, are equally applicable in global research situations as they are in conjunction with domestic projects. ESOMAR's code of ethics is provided in its entirety in Appendix 2.

While the code spells out expectations for both clients and market research suppliers in great detail, this general summary covers the key points:[1]

- Research should be conducted objectively and follow established principles.

- Research must adhere to the laws of the countries in which it is conducted.

- Respondents must participate voluntarily in the research study.

- Respondents' personal information/identities must be kept confidential.

- Respondents must be kept safe during their participation in a study.

- Parental consent is required to interview children.

- You must let respondents know if interviews are recorded/observed.

- Respondents should be able to confirm that the research project/supplier is legitimate.

- Suppliers cannot mislead/lie about their research capabilities.

- Suppliers cannot speak badly about other suppliers.

- Projects should be cost-efficient and meet quality standards.

- Suppliers must keep all records safe and confidential.

- Suppliers should not offer conclusions that are not supported by research data and must clearly separate actual findings from recommendations.

- Suppliers cannot use data/sample for purposes unrelated to the research for which it is intended.

- Suppliers should inform clients if their study is conducted as part of syndicated work including other clients.

- Suppliers must disclose if they are subcontracting any of the client's research.

- The client owns the RFP and any other materials provided to the research supplier as well as all data/findings from their specific project (with the exception of the names and contact information of the respondents).
- Suppliers own the research proposals/bids.
- Suppliers must maintain research project records for an appropriate time period.
- Suppliers must not tell any third party who their clients are without the permission of those clients.
- Clients must be allowed to check the quality of fieldwork and data (but must pay the related costs to do so).
- Suppliers must provide all technical details of the clients' projects.
- Clients must be sure that any findings from the research they publish must not be misleading.

As in any business relationship, ethics generally rely on common sense. Basic guidelines include the following:

- Be forthcoming. Trust your research supplier and be professional.
- Be genuine. Don't ask for a proposal you do not actually expect to give serious consideration to.
- Negotiate pricing fairly.

- Do not promise what you can't provide.
- Provide all research suppliers with the same information.

Trust Your Supplier

Be forthcoming. Trust your research supplier and be professional.

It is perfectly acceptable to ask your suppliers (even during the proposal phase) to complete and sign nondisclosure documents to legally ensure the confidentiality of your research. This is actually a good practice, particularly if your research is related to a new product concept you cannot risk competitors hearing about in advance.

Requesting a nondisclosure document is not an indicator of mistrust, but rather a sound business practice. Once this agreement is signed, however, you should trust your supplier to maintain the agreed-upon confidentiality and move on with the research. Research vendors may very likely have several clients in the same industry and possibly even direct competitors. It would certainly not be in a vendor's best interests to divulge information about one client to another.

Likewise, it is neither professional nor realistic for you as the client to insist that the vendor not conduct research for other companies in your industry. Provided that different project managers are handling competitors' projects there should not be any reason to worry about project security.

Some technology clients will go so far as to conduct security checks at their vendor's offices to ensure that confidential information is properly secured (i.e., documentation is not sitting on desktops, prototypes are not laying around, and data is not easily viewed on a computer monitor on the manager's desk). With a new vendor, you may wish to do this. Where you have an ongoing relationship with the research supplier, however, you should have established a sense of trust and not need to check up on security for each project, although a periodic check might be in order, particularly if there have been important staff changes.

Furthermore on the subject of trust, both you and the supplier-side manager need to be able to address issues that arise promptly and without trying to "sugarcoat" problems. The sooner a problem such as under-recruited focus groups, questionnaire design errors or other similar issues are dealt with, the less dire the effects of the problem on your research. By openly and immediately dealing with any problems, you will save money and time and ultimately be more likely to ensure the integrity of your final research results.

Take a look at Example 12.1 to see how a concern about a competitive issue was handled.

Example 12.1
HANDLING THE COMPETITION

Situation: Your research supplier works for one of your key competitors and has made you aware of this early in your proposal process. Nonetheless, your manager and others on your research team are concerned that the highly confidential new product concepts which you are testing globally may somehow fall into the wrong hands.

Solution: You have gone to great lengths during the vendor selection process to ensure that your vendor has a good and ethical reputation. Be open with your primary vendor contact and stress again the confidentiality concerns, not insinuating distrust, but rather that given the number of people involved in the study, it is natural for management to worry. Then provide a nondisclosure agreement that will serve to protect your firm's intellectual property.

Be Serious

Be genuine. Don't ask for a proposal you do not actually expect to give serious consideration to.

It is not reasonable to expect a research vendor to spend time and to incur expenses in order to provide you with a thorough proposal if you are not truly planning to consider its proposal for your project.

Many large corporations require their managers to obtain several bids before they are able to select a research provider and award the project. This is a reasonable expectation and is helpful in providing you with a range of estimated costs as well as potential methodology options for your study.

If, however, you already have predetermined that you will used a "tried and true" research supplier regardless of what other competitors propose, then you are unfairly using the system and taking advantage of the other vendors to get around your own corporate red tape. See Example 12.2.

Negotiating Price

Negotiate pricing fairly. While you should expect to pay a fair price for the services, likewise the research vendor should be expected to be able to make a fair profit on the work it is doing for you. Be cautious not to ask for the world (pun intended) with only a domestic budget available for this research study. Example 12.3 addresses this issue.

Setting Realistic Expectations

Do not promise what you can't provide. If you are unable to provide any information for use in the study (i.e., sample lists, sales figures, etc., do not even hint that you may be able to do so.

Research suppliers develop their cost estimates for your project based on the information you have provided to them in your RFP. If you lead them to expect that sam-

Example 12.2
CHOOSING VENDORS

Situation: Your manager has asked you to "bid out" a large research tracking study which will be conducted in several countries. You have one vendor which you use frequently and another which has a strong reputation for international tracking studies. Unfortunately, your purchasing process requires that you send out for three independent bids on a study of this size.

Solution: You basically have two options in this situation. First, if you will honestly consider another firm's bid, make every effort to identify a third market research supplier which is qualified to bid on this type of study. If this is not a possibility, you should discuss this concern with your manager and/or the purchasing department to determine if you can be allowed to select a vendor based on the two firms from whom you want to get proposals.

In a worst case scenario, if you must find a third vendor to bid, but are not serious about considering that vendor for the research, be open with the vendor and advise the vendor that you cannot consider their bid this time, but require it for internal procedures. Then tell them you would be willing to consider them for another project when the chance arises

This may provide adequate incentive for the firm to bid as it allows the first to at least get their capabilities in front of you for future opportunities.

Example 12.3
NEGOTIATING FOR SERVICES

Situation: You have received three proposals for your upcoming international research project and all of them are substantially more expensive than you had anticipated. You need to get the research done quickly and do not have any means of obtaining extra funding in time for this particular study.

Solution: You should approach all of the bidding vendors and explain your predicament with the budget. Ask if they can suggest options which would allow you to meet your objectives while staying within your budget. Do not expect them to cut their prices simply because you need them to! They should be able to suggest some ways to accomplish the research in a more cost-effective manner, such as cutting a region, decreasing sample sizes or possibly doing the study in two parts so that you can pay for the second part of the study during the next budget period.

ple lists or other pertinent information for use in your study will be provided, they generally will expect this to be a certainty. They will not typically provide estimates for these services or, still worse, may not have a comparable solution if you end up being unable to provide the promised information. Example 12.4 suggests a way to handle this.

Example 12.4
DEVELOPING COST ESTIMATES

Situation: You have selected a vendor and are finalizing the questionnaire with the project manager. The topic of the sample comes up as fielding is scheduled to start the next week. The project manager asks when you are going to have the contact lists for the study and you realize that they expect you to provide them because in your RFP you mentioned they would be available for use as a sample. Unfortunately, the lists are not current and cannot be used after all.

Solution: You should explain the situation to the vendor and discuss other sampling options at this point in time. Be prepared to pay for the sample and possibly more per interview, as the list you eventually end up with may not be as reliable as what the vendor was expecting you to provide. The cost per interview may increase should the incidence be substantially lower than what was estimated based on the promise of your contact lists.

Consistent RFP

Provide all research suppliers with the same information. As mentioned previously, you should provide each of the vendors who are being invited to bid on your research project with the identical version of your RFP. Furthermore, if any vendor approaches you with questions regarding your RFP, you should answer the questions for all vendors, whether or not they make any inquiries about the RFP themselves. As stated earlier, this will "level the playing field" for all of the research vendors involved, but just as importantly, it will guarantee that you will be able to easily make comparisons between the proposals you receive as the suppliers are all certain to be bidding based on the same specifications and assumptions. If you did not handle it this way when the query came in, you have an opportunity to remedy this, as described in Example 12.5.

Example 12.5
STRUCTURING AN RFP

Situation: You have sent an RFP for a quantitative research study to four research suppliers. During the process of writing their proposals, one of the vendors contacts you regarding any prior research that might have been done on the research subject matter. You mention that recently a series of focus groups had been conducted on this topic, and the vendor is enthusiastic because the results of that study will help in the development of the questionnaire for the survey they are bidding on. You do not, however, pass this same information on to the other three vendors. When the completed proposals reach your desk, the vendor who made the initial inquiry about prior research has provided a lower bid, particularly in the design phase of the proposed study.

Solution: In order to allow for a fair bid process, you should now notify the three vendors who did not receive the advance information regarding the prior qualitative research study. Offer them an opportunity to revise their bids if they feel this will in any way change their initial estimates. Once they provide the revised costs or opt to keep their proposals the same, you can make a fair assessment of the proposals.

Chapter 12 Take-Aways

☑ Ethics play a crucial role when conducting an international research project.

☑ A number of organizations offer ethical guidelines or codes for research:

- CASRO (Council of American Survey Research Organizations)
- MRA (Market Research Association)
- ESOMAR (European Society for Opinion and Marketing Research)

☑ General guidelines include the following:

- Be forthcoming—trust your supplier and be professional.
- Be genuine—don't ask for a proposal you do not plan to consider.
- Negotiate pricing fairly.
- Do not promise to provide information that you are not positive you will be able to provide.
- Provide all suppliers who receive your RFP with the same information.

Glossary of Terms

active briefing—process of having local vendor team reiterate in their own words their tasks and responsibilities for the research project as they understand them, following the initial briefing with the client.

AMA—American Marketing Association.

back translation—a two-way translation process where a questionnaire is translated first into the required survey language and then translated back from that language into the native language to check on the quality of the translation.

banner—headings used in data tables of survey results.

briefing—session during which interviewers, supervisors, focus group moderators and/or interpreters are trained regarding the research objectives, screener(s), questionnaire(s) and discussion guide(s) prior to the fieldwork start-up for a research study.

C-level—term used to designate high-level executives (i.e., CEO, CFO, CIO, etc.).

CAPI—computer-aided personal interviewing; an interviewer is present to answer questions as appropriate, but the respondent completes an in-person interview on the computer.

CASRO—Council of American Survey Research Organizations.

CATI—computer-aided telephone interviewing; the questionnaire and the prompts/interviewer instructions are programmed for telephone interviewers to follow on screen.

Choice-based analysis—a form of conjoint analysis that provides models based on real-life consumer behavior.

Conjoint analysis—a multivariate survey technique in which respondents trade product features/attributes against each other; helps to determine brand preference and features' relative importance; allows development of market simulators.

cooperative payment—see "incentive."

cost per interview (CPI)—the cost per completed recruit or survey interview based on total sample size of the study and fieldwork costs; firms may include different costs in this calculation.

credentials—detailed background information and references offered by a research supplier to clients (can be separate or included in a proposal).

cross-tabulations—survey question responses sorted and tallied by the responses given to one or more other selected survey question(s) such as age, gender, country, income level, etc.

data collection—process of gathering research data inputs (i.e., via telephone, mail, Web, etc.).

data processing—computer analysis of data resulting from research responses.

debriefing—a discussion between the client and vendor teams that immediately follows a focus group or series of interviews; generally pertains to how well the study is meeting the proposed objectives and/or how well the respondents understand what is being asked.

deliverables—those items the research supplier is to provide to the client over the course of a project; i.e., screeners, questionnaires, discussion guides, reports, presentation, etc.

depth interviews—interviews (either face-to-face or by phone) that are more qualitative than quantitative in nature.

discussion guide—outline used by a focus group moderator to guide the course of the discussion and ensure that all of the research objectives are covered.

dyad—a qualitative research discussion conducted by a moderator with only two participants.

ESOMAR—European Society for Opinion and Marketing Research.

fieldwork—the actual process of screening, focus group/depth-interview recruiting, or survey interviewing for a market research project.

focus group—a qualitative research discussion group led by a moderator.

focus group participant—a person who has been recruited and attends a focus group session with the intent to provide inputs and participate in the research discussion.

focus group transcript—word-for-word quotation of research participants in response to specific questions in focus group sessions that are taken from audio and/or videotapes.

ICC—an acronym for the International Chamber of Commerce.

incentive—compensation to respondents in form of a check, cash, entry into a prize drawing, charitable donations, etc.

incidence—the percentage of qualified respondents/participants within the population being contacted.

interviewer—the person who conducts a research survey following a pre-designed questionnaire.

kick-off meeting—the initial meeting conducted between client and research supplier once the project is commissioned.

list broker—the company which pulls and distributes lists based on specific requests; generally for sales or research purposes; see also sample provider.

methodology—the means by which a research study is conducted (i.e., mail, mystery shops, focus groups, etc.) as well as the type of study (i.e., conjoint analysis, Simalto, choice-based analysis, etc.).

moderator—a focus group facilitator whose main role is to keep the discussion on track and to elicit comments related to meeting the study's research objectives.

monitoring—listening to survey interviews with the respondent unaware; conducted from a viewing room for one-on-one depth interviews or by phone during telephone interviews.

MRA—Market Research Association.

MRS—the UK Market Research Society (*www.mrs.org. uk*).

mystery shop—research study in which interviewers play the role of customers and "shop" at a specific bank, store, etc., with the objective being to test sales and service.

NDA—nondisclosure agreement; generally signed by the research supplier and occasionally by interviewers and/or focus group participants to emphasize the confidential nature of the research subject matter and ensure that they will not discuss the project, client and/or products/services being discussed outside of the client/vendor relationship.

panel—a base of respondents who receive prizes or are awarded points for participating in a survey and pre-recruited by a research supplier to be contacted for client surveys on an as-needed basis determined by their responses to initial respondent profiles and screeners.

PDA—abbreviation for personal digital assistant; palm-held devices with email, calendars, contact information and other organizational capabilities.

primary research—quantitative or qualitative research not conducted prior to the proposed research, but designed specifically to meet the predetermined objectives of a client.

QRCA—Qualitative Research Consultants Association.

qualitative research—a relatively unstructured form of research, i.e., focus groups, one-on-one depth interviews, etc., the results of which are interpreted subjectively and usually include a number of direct quotations from respondents/participants.

quantitative research—a structured survey research method which is designed to provide statistically valid results which can be graphically represented.

questionnaire—a structured series of questions used in conducting a research interview.

quota—a set number of interviews required within a given target category, e.g., percentage of respondents that must fall into a specific household income range category.

recruitment—the process of screening and inviting participants to take part in a research study; generally done via telephone for focus groups or in-depth interviews.

Request for Proposal (RFP)—document sent to research suppliers providing project specifications and defining business objectives for a potential research study; its purpose is to result in a formal proposal from said suppliers.

Request for Qualifications (RFQ)—a request for credentials sent from a client to a research vendor; generally exploratory in nature to narrow down potential vendors prior to sending out an RFP.

research facility—a site where telephone surveys are conducted or where purpose-built focus group and client viewing rooms are located.

research objectives—the key issues about which the client wants to learn answers from the research study.

research respondent—a person who is qualified to answer research survey questions based on qualifying through one or more screening questions.

sample—list of contact names used to recruit focus group participants or to screen survey respondents; lists may vary by what information they include, i.e., contact name, title, telephone number, address, email address, etc.

sample provider—a firm which sells lists for use in research studies.

screener—brief questionnaire that determines if a targeted respondent is qualified to participate in a research study.

secondary research—data which is already available for review and does not require a new survey or study to gather (i.e., census data, prior research study results, syndicated research reports available for purchase, etc.).

Simalto—ShareSim® Simalto is an extremely flexible primary research-based methodology for analyzing and predicting customer wants, needs and preferences in complex decision/choice situations; a tool for matching a client's products, service and image as closely as possible with customer priorities and values in order to maximize market share potential, get the best return on investment, and increase customer loyalty/preference.

simultaneous interpretation—process by which an interpreter translates focus group conversations in real time from the language the group is using into the native language of the client company's team.

specifications—the details of what a research study is expected to include, i.e., targeted respondents, countries/regions, objectives to be met, timeline for the study, etc.

SPSS—software for research data collection and analysis (see *www.spss.com*).

syndicated research—research conducted by firms, the results of which are compiled into reports and sold to provide companies with general information about an industry, segment of the population, etc.

target respondents—people within a segment of the market to which a marketer directs an advertising campaign, marketing program, promotion or product and who will be researched.

telephone interviews—survey interviews conducted by telephone.

top-line—the initial results of a study, provided prior to any formal analysis.

triad—a qualitative research discussion conducted by a moderator with three participants.

validation—process by which respondents to a survey are re-contacted by a research supplier to ensure that they did actually give the responses recorded by the research interviewer; a service quality process.

verbatim—word-for-word quotation of a research participant's response to a specific question or comment.

viewing room—a small room outside of the focus group room where clients are able to view the focus groups while they are being conducted; viewing is generally via a one-way mirror with sound provided via an intercom system.

Appendix 1
Holidays in Selected Countries

The following list[1] includes the majority of nationally recognized holidays which occur on set dates in the countries of Argentina, Brazil, China, England, France, Germany, India, Italy, Japan, Mexico, Russia, South Korea, and the United States:

Jan. 1:   Argentina (New Year's Day)

            Brazil (New Year's Day)

            People's Republic of China (New Year's Day)

            England (New Year's Day)

            France (New Year's Day)

            Germany (New Year's Day)

            India (New Year's Day)

            Italy (New Year's Day)

            Mexico (New Year's Day)

            Russia (New Year)

            South Korea (New Year's Day)

            United States (New Year's Day)

Jan. 2:   Russia (New Year)

Jan. 6:	Germany (Epiphany)
	Italy (Epiphany)
Jan. 7:	Russia (Christmas in Russian Orthodox Church)
Jan. 20:	Brazil (St. Sebastian—Rio de Janeiro only)
Jan. 25:	Brazil (Founding of Sao Paulo—Sao Paulo only)
Jan. 26:	India (Republic Day)
Feb. 5:	Mexico (Constitution Day)
Feb. 11:	Japan (National Foundation Day)
Feb. 23:	Russia (Day of the Defenders of the Motherland)
March 1:	South Korea (Independence Movement Day)
March 8:	Russia (International Women's Day)
March 21:	Mexico (Benito Juarez's Birthday)
March 25:	England (Good Friday)
April 2:	Argentina (Veterans' Day)
April 5:	South Korea (Arbor Day)
April 8:	Japan (Flower Festival—Buddha's Birthday)
April 21:	Brazil (Tiradentes)
April 23:	Brazil (St. George—only in Rio de Janeiro)
April 25:	Italy (Anniversary of Liberation)
April 29:	Japan (Greenery Day)
May 1:	Argentina (Labor Day)
	Brazil (Labor Day)
	People's Republic of China (Labor Day)
	France (Labor Day)
	Germany (May Day)
	India (Labor Day)

Italy (Labor Day)

Mexico (Labor Day)

Russia (Labor Day/Celebration of Spring—continues on May 2nd)

May 3: Japan (Constitution Memorial Day)

May 4: People's Republic of China (Youth Day)

Japan (Between Day)

May 5: Japan (Children's Day)

South Korea (Children's Day)

Mexico (Cinco de Mayo)

May 8: France (V-E Day)

May 9: Russia (Victory Day)

May 25: Argentina (Anniversary of the First Independent Government in Buenos Aires)

June 2: Italy (Republic Day)

June 6: South Korea (Memorial Day)

June 12: Russia (Independence Day)

June 20: Argentina (National Flag Day)

Brazil (Constitutionalist Revolution—Sao Paolo only)

July 1: People's Republic of China (CPC Founding Day)

July 4: United States (Independence Day)

July 9: Argentina (National Independence Day)

July 14: France (Bastille Day)

July 17: South Korea (Constitution Day)

Aug. 1: People's Republic of China (Army Day)

Aug. 15: France (Assumption Day)

Germany (Assumption Day)

India (Independence Day)

Italy (Assumption Day)

South Korea (Independence Day)

Aug. 17: Argentina (Anniversary of Death of General Jose de San Martin)

Sept. 7: Brazil (Independence Day)

Sept. 11: Argentina (Teachers' Day)

Sept. 16: Mexico (Independence Day)

Sept. 21: Argentina (Students' Day)

Oct. 1: People's Republic of China (National Day)

Oct. 2: India (Birthday of Mahatma Gandhi)

Oct. 3: Germany (German Unity Day)

South Korea (National Foundation Day)

Oct. 12: Argentina (Columbus Day)

Brazil (Our Lady of Aparecida)

Oct. 31: Germany (Reformation Day)

Nov. 1: France (All Saints Day)

Germany (All Saints Day)

Italy (All Saints Day)

Nov. 2: Brazil (All Souls Day)

Nov. 3: Japan (Culture Day)

Nov. 7: Russia (Day of Accord and Reconciliation)

Nov. 11: France (Remembrance Day, Veterans' Day, Armistice Day)

United States (Veterans' Day)

Nov. 15: Brazil (Proclamation of the Republic Day)

Nov. 20: Brazil (Zumbi of Palmares, Black Consciousness Day, Rio de Janeiro only)

Mexico (Revolution Day)

Nov. 23:   Japan (Labor Thanksgiving Day)

Dec. 8:   Argentina (Immaculate Conception Day)

Italy (Immaculate Conception)

Dec. 12:   Russia (Constitution Day)

Dec. 23:   Japan (The Emperor's Birthday)

Dec. 24:   Argentina (Christmas Eve)

Dec. 25:   Argentina (Christmas Day)

Brazil (Christmas Day)

England (Christmas Day)

France (Christmas Day)

Germany (Christmas Day)

Italy (Christmas Day)

Mexico (Christmas Day)

South Korea (Christmas Day)

United States (Christmas Day)

Dec. 26:   England (Boxing Day)

Germany (Boxing Day)

Italy (St. Stephen's Day)

Note that nearly all of these countries have floating nationally recognized holidays as well or holidays that occur in conjunction with non-Westernized calendars. Some examples include:

Argentina: Good Friday

Brazil: Carnival (Tuesday before Ash Wednesday), Ash Wednesday, Good Friday, Corpus Christi (62 days after Good Friday)

China: A number of festivals based on the

219

Chinese calendar—Spring Festival (Chinese New Year), Lantern Festival, Tomb Sweeping Day, Dragon Boat Festival, Double Seven Festival (similar to Valentine's Day), Spirit Festival, Mid-Autumn Festival (Moon Festival), and Double Ninth Festival

England: Good Friday, Easter Monday, Early May Bank Holiday, Spring Bank Holiday (end of May), Summer Bank Holiday (end of August)

France: Easter, Easter Monday, Ascension Day (Thursday, 40 days after Easter), Pentecost (seventh Sunday after Easter)

Germany: Good Friday, Easter Monday, Ascension Day, Whitmonday, Corpus Christi

Italy: Easter Sunday, Easter Monday

Japan: Shogatsu (the first half of January celebrating the New Year), Coming-of-Age Day (second Monday of January), Vernal equinox (around March 21st), Marine Day (third Monday of July), Respect for the Aged Day (third Monday of September), Autumnal equinox (around September 23rd), Health and Sports Day (Second Monday of October)

South Korea: A number of holidays based on the lunar calendar—Lunar New Year's Day (1st month, 1st day—usually in early February), Buddha's Birthday (4th month, 8th day—usually in late May), Thanksgiving Day (8th month, 15th day—usually in late September)

United States: Martin Luther King Day (third Monday of January), President's Day (third Monday of February), Memorial Day (last Monday of May), Labor Day (first Monday after the first Sunday in September), Columbus Day (second Monday of October), Thanksgiving Day (fourth Thursday of November)

Appendix 2
Research Ethics Code

ICC/ESOMAR:

**ICC/ESOMAR International Code of Marketing and
  Social Research Practice**

Introduction

Definitions

Rules

Notes on applying the ICC/ESOMAR International Code
  (2001)

Annexe to Notes

Introduction

Effective communication between the suppliers and the
consumers of goods and services of all kinds is vital to
any modern society. Growing international links make
this even more essential. For a supplier to provide in the
most efficient way what consumers require he must understand their differing needs; how best to meet these

needs; and how he can most effectively communicate the nature of the goods or services he is offering.

This is the objective of marketing research. It applies in both private and public sectors of the economy. Similar approaches are also used in other fields of study: for example in measuring the public's behaviour and attitudes with respect to social, political and other issues by Government and public bodies, the media, academic institutions, etc. Marketing and social research have many interests, methods and problems in common although the subjects of study tend to be different.

Such research depends upon public confidence: confidence that it is carried out honestly, objectively, without unwelcome intrusion or disadvantage to respondents, and that it is based upon their willing cooperation. This confidence must be supported by an appropriate professional Code of Practice which governs the way in which marketing research projects are conducted.

The first such Code was published by ESOMAR in 1948. This was followed by a number of Codes prepared by national marketing research societies and by other bodies such as the International Chamber of Commerce (ICC), which represents the international marketing community. In 1976 ESOMAR and the ICC decided that it would be preferable to have a single International Code instead of two differing ones, and a joint ICC/ESOMAR Code was therefore published in the following year (with revisions in 1986).

Subsequent changes in the marketing and social environment, new developments in marketing research methods and a great increase in international activities of all kinds including legislation, led ESOMAR to prepare a new version of the International Code in 1994. This new version sets out as concisely as possible the basic ethical and business principles which govern the practice of marketing and social research. It specifies the rules which are to be followed in dealing with the general public and with the business community, including clients and other members of the profession.

ESOMAR will be glad to give advice on the implementation of this Code; and also offers an arbitration and expert assessment service to help resolve technical and other disputes relating to marketing research projects.

Other aspects of marketing—in particular Direct Marketing and Advertising—are covered by separate International Codes of Practice published by the ICC. Copies of these may be obtained from the ICC Secretariat in Paris.

The International Code

This Code sets out the basic principles which must guide the actions of those who carry out or use marketing research. Individuals and organisations who subscribe to it must follow not just the letter but also the spirit of these rules.

No Code can be expected to provide a completely comprehensive set of rules which are applicable to every situation which might arise. Where there is any element of doubt people should ask for advice and meanwhile follow the most conservative interpretation of these principles. No variation in the application of the rules is permissible without explicit authorisation by ESOMAR and ICC.

In certain countries there are additional national requirements laid down by legislation or by the local professional association which may affect the application of the International Code. Where they add to or differ from those set out in this Code such specific national requirements take precedence when carrying out research [1] in that country. This applies to all research in that country even when it is carried out by researchers or clients based elsewhere. National associations can provide information on any special requirements of these kinds which must be observed in their own country.

Individuals are always responsible for ensuring that the other people in their organisation who to their knowledge are concerned in any way with marketing research activities are aware of, and understand, the principles laid down in this Code. They must use their best endeavours to ensure that the organisation as a whole conforms to the Code.

Acceptance of this International Code is a condition of membership of ESOMAR and of all other national and international bodies which have officially adopted the Code. Members should also familiarise themselves with the Notes and Guidelines which ESOMAR produces to help in interpreting and applying the Rules of this Code.

Definitions

(a) **Marketing research** is a key element within the total field of marketing information. It links the consumer, customer and public to the marketer through information which is used to identify and define marketing opportunities and problems; generate, refine and evaluate marketing actions; improve understanding of marketing as a process and of the ways in which specific marketing activities can be made more effective.

Marketing research specifies the information required to address these issues; designs the method for collecting information; manages and implements the data collection process; analyses the results; and communicates the findings and their implications.

Marketing research includes such activities as quantitative surveys; qualitative research; media and advertising research; business-to-business and industrial research; research among minority and special groups; public opinion surveys; and desk research.

In the context of this Code the term marketing research also covers social research where this uses similar approaches and techniques to study issues not concerned with the marketing of goods and services. The applied social sciences equally depend upon such methods of empirical research to develop and test their underlying hypotheses; and to understand, predict and provide guidance on developments within society for governmental, academic and other purposes.

Marketing research differs from other forms of information gathering in that the identity of the provider of information is not disclosed. Database marketing and any other activity where the names and addresses of the people contacted are to be used for individual selling, promotional, fund-raising or other non-research purposes can under no circumstances be regarded as marketing research since the latter is based on preserving the complete anonymity of the respondent.

(b) **Researcher** is defined as any individual, research agency, organisation, department or division which carries out or acts as a consultant on a marketing research project or offers their services so to do.

The term includes any department etc. which belongs to the same organisation as that of the client. A researcher linked to the client in this way has the same responsibilities under this Code *vis-à-vis* other sections of the client organisation as does one who is completely independent of the latter.

The term also covers responsibility for the procedures followed by any subcontractor from whom the researcher commissions any work (data collection or analysis, printing, professional consultancy, etc.) which forms any part of the research project. In such cases the researcher must ensure that any such subcontractor fully conforms to the provisions of this Code.

(c) **Client** is defined as any individual, organisation, department or division (including one which belongs to the same organisation as the researcher) which requests, commissions or subscribes to all or any part of a marketing research project.

(d) **Respondent** is defined as any individual or organisation from whom any information is sought by the researcher for the purposes of a marketing research project. The term covers cases where information is to be obtained by verbal interviewing techniques, postal and other self-completion questionnaires, mechanical or electronic equipment, observation and any other method where the identity of the provider of the information may be recorded or otherwise traceable.

(e) **Interview** is defined as any form of direct or indirect contact, using any of the methods referred to above, with respondents where the objective is to acquire data or information which could be used in whole or in part for the purposes of a marketing research project.

(f) **Record** is defined as any brief, proposal, questionnaire, respondent identification, check list, record sheet, audio or audio-visual recording or film, tabulation or computer print-out, EDP disc or other storage medium, formula, diagram, report, etc. in respect of any marketing research project, whether in whole or in part. It covers records produced by the client as well as by the researcher.

Rules

A. General

1. Marketing research must always be carried out objectively and in accordance with established scientific principles.

2. Marketing research must always conform to the national and international legislation which applies in those countries involved in a given research project.

B. The Rights of Respondents

3. Respondents' cooperation in a marketing research project is entirely voluntary at all stages. They must not be misled when being asked for their cooperation.

4. Respondents' anonymity must be strictly preserved. If the Respondent on request from the Researcher has given permission for data to be passed on in a form which allows that Respondent to be personally identified:
(a) the Respondent must first have been told to whom the information would be supplied and the purposes for which it will be used, and also
(b) the Researcher must ensure that the information will not be used for any non-research purpose and that the recipient of the information has agreed to conform to the requirements of this Code.

5. The Researcher must take all reasonable precautions to ensure that Respondents are in no way directly harmed or

adversely affected as a result of their participation in a marketing research project.

6. The Researcher must take special care when interviewing children and young people. The informed consent of the parent or responsible adult must first be obtained for interviews with children.

7. Respondents must be told (normally at the beginning of the interview) if observation techniques or recording equipment are being used, except where these are used in a public place. If a Respondent so wishes, the record or relevant section of it must be destroyed or deleted. Respondents' anonymity must not be infringed by the use of such methods.

8. Respondents must be enabled to check without difficulty the identity and bona fides of the Researcher.

C. The Professional Responsibilities of Researchers

9. Researchers must not, whether knowingly or negligently, act in any way which could bring discredit on the marketing research profession or lead to a loss of public confidence in it.

10. Researchers must not make false claims about their skills and experience or about those of their organisation.

11. Researchers must not unjustifiably criticise or disparage other Researchers.

12. Researchers must always strive to design research

which is cost-efficient and of adequate quality, and then to carry this out to the specifications agreed with the Client.

13. Researchers must ensure the security of all research records in their possession.

14. Researchers must not knowingly allow the dissemination of conclusions from a marketing research project which are not adequately supported by the data. They must always be prepared to make available the technical information necessary to assess the validity of any published findings.

15. When acting in their capacity as Researchers the latter must not undertake any non-research activities, for example database marketing involving data about individuals which will be used for direct marketing and promotional activities. Any such non-research activities must always, in the way they are organised and carried out, be clearly differentiated from marketing research activities.

D. The Mutual Rights and Responsibilities of Researchers and Clients

16. These rights and responsibilities will normally be governed by a written Contract between the Researcher and the Client. The parties may amend the provisions of Rules 19–23 below if they have agreed to this in writing beforehand; but the other requirements of this Code may not be altered in this way. Marketing research must also always

be conducted according to the principles of fair competition, as generally understood and accepted.

17. The Researcher must inform the Client if the work to be carried out for that Client is to be combined or syndicated in the same project with work for other Clients but must not disclose the identity of such Clients.

18. The Researcher must inform the Client as soon as possible in advance when any part of the work for that Client is to be subcontracted outside the Researcher's own organisation (including the use of any outside consultants). On request the Client must be told the identity of any such subcontractor.

19. The Client does not have the right, without prior agreement between the parties involved, to exclusive use of the Researcher's services or those of his organisation, whether in whole or in part. In carrying out work for different Clients, however, the Researcher must endeavour to avoid possible clashes of interest between the services provided to those Clients.

20. The following Records remain the property of the Client and must not be disclosed by the Researcher to any third party without the Client's permission:

(a) Marketing research briefs, specifications and other information provided by the Client.

(b) The research data and findings from a marketing research project (except in the case of syndicated or multi-client projects or services where the same data are available to more than one Client).

The Client has however no right to know the names or addresses of Respondents unless the latter's explicit permission for this has first been obtained by the Researcher (this particular requirement cannot be altered under Rule 16).

21. Unless it is specifically agreed to the contrary, the following Records remain the property of the Researcher:

(a) Marketing research proposals and cost quotations (unless these have been paid for by the Client). They must not be disclosed by the Client to any third party, other than to a consultant working for the Client on that project (with the exception of any consultant working also for a competitor of the Researcher). In particular, they must not be used by the Client to influence research proposals or cost quotations from other Researchers.

(b) The contents of a report in the case of syndicated and/or multi-client projects or services where the same data are available to more than one Client and where it is clearly understood that the resulting reports are available for general purchase or subscription. The Client may not disclose the findings of such research to any third party (other than to his own consultants and advisors for use in connection with his business) without the permission of the Researcher.

(c) All other research Records prepared by the Researcher (with the exception in the case of non-syndicated projects of the report to the Client, and also the research design and questionnaire where the costs of developing these are covered by the charges paid by the Client).

22. The Researcher must conform to currently agreed professional practice relating to the keeping of such Records for an appropriate period of time after the end of the project. On request the Researcher must supply the Client with duplicate copies of such Records provided that such duplicates do not breach anonymity and confidentiality requirements (Rule 4); that the request is made within the agreed time limit for keeping the Records; and that the Client pays the reasonable costs of providing the duplicates.

23. The Researcher must not disclose the identity of the Client (provided there is no legal obligation to do so), or any confidential information about the latter's business, to any third party without the Client's permission.

24. The Researcher must on request allow the Client to arrange for checks on the quality of fieldwork and data preparation provided that the Client pays any additional costs involved in this. Any such checks must conform to the requirements of Rule 4.

25. The Researcher must provide the Client with all appropriate technical details of any research project carried out for that Client.

26. When reporting on the results of a marketing research project the Researcher must make a clear distinction

between the findings as such, the Researcher's interpretation of these and any recommendations based on them.

27. Where any of the findings of a research project are published by the Client the latter has a responsibility to ensure that these are not misleading. The Researcher must be consulted and agree in advance the form and content of publication, and must take action to correct any misleading statements about the research and its findings.

28. Researchers must not allow their names to be used in connection with any research project as an assurance that the latter has been carried out in conformity with this Code unless they are confident that the project has in all respects met the Code's requirements.

29. Researchers must ensure that Clients are aware of the existence of this Code and of the need to comply with its requirements.

E. Implementation of the Code

Queries about the interpretation of this Code, and about its application to specific problems, should be addressed to the international Secretariats of the ICC or ESOMAR.

Any apparent infringement, if it applies solely to activities within a single country, should in the first place be reported immediately to the appropriate national body (or bodies) in that country. A list of such bodies which have adopted this Code will be found in the Appendix. That national body will then investigate and take any appropriate action, notifying the ICC/ESOMAR of the outcome in the case of proven infringement.

Apparent infringements should be reported directly to the Secretariats of the ICC or ESOMAR in cases where:

(a) there is no appropriate national body,

(b) the national body is unable to take action or prefers the issue to be dealt with by the international body,

(c) more than one country is involved, as with international projects.

Notes on applying the ICC/ESOMAR International Code (2001)

Introduction

These notes are designed by ESOMAR to help users of the International Code to interpret and apply it in practice. Any further questions about the Code, for example on how to apply it in a specific situation, should be addressed to the Secretariats of ESOMAR or the ICC, as appropriate.

The notes will be reviewed periodically to take account of changing circumstances or important new issues. When necessary, further editions will be published by ESOMAR after consultation with the ICC and with other relevant bodies.

The ICC has also published other Codes of Practice which cover a variety of marketing issues not addressed in the ICC/ESOMAR International Code. In particular, the

ICC's Code on Direct Marketing deals with the different requirements which apply to that separate field of marketing activity.

Section A: General

(RULE 2)

This Rule requires that Researchers must always conform to the requirements of international and national legislation. Whenever national or international law imposes obligations in any given country which are more onerous than those already imposed by the ICC/ESOMAR Code, as elaborated in these Notes, Researchers must comply with these stricter obligations.[*]

One very important element of legislation relates to data protection. The European Data Protection Directive, and the national legislation stemming from it, sets out the requirements which must be complied with by Researchers based or carrying out research in the EU, or handling personal data collected within the EU. The key implications of such legislation for marketing research, including social and opinion research, are covered in the present Notes. However, for more detailed guidance on what is required by the Directive when dealing with research in the EU, readers are referred to, and must comply with, the special ESOMAR "Annexe to Notes on the ICC/ESOMAR International Code" which describes the EU Data Protection requirements. Where researchers have questions on detailed local issues they should also refer to the relevant national marketing research associations for further advice on current national data protection requirements in the countries in which they plan to carry out research.

Marketing research conducted according to the principles of transparency, confidentiality and secure handling of personal data has achieved growing recognition as a form of "statistical or scientific research" since personalised information cannot be disclosed for non-research purposes such as direct marketing. This guarantees the confidential nature of marketing research data. Such recognition must not be jeopardised by any failure to conform to these principles.

---

*Readers' attention is called to the fact that the German-language version of the International Code is prefaced by a Declaration prepared by the German national market research associations. This sets out certain additional requirements which must be followed in order to conform with German legislation when carrying out research in that country. Copies of this Declaration are available on request from the ESOMAR Secretariat, in the following languages—English, French, German and Spanish.

Section B: The Rights of Respondents

All Respondents are entitled to be sure that when they voluntarily agree to cooperate in a marketing research project they will be fully protected by the provisions of the ICC/ESOMAR International Code, as elaborated by these Notes, as well as by the relevant provisions of national and international law. This applies equally to Respondents interviewed as private individuals and to those interviewed as representatives of organisations of different kinds.

The EU Data Protection Directive covers only "personal data," defined as information relating to identified or identifiable natural persons. An "identifiable person" is someone whose identity can be determined either directly (for example by name, address or identity number) or indirectly by information concerning the person's physical, physiological, mental, economic, cultural or social characteristics. This includes audio and visual material such as tapes, film or video recordings.

The Directive requirements mean *inter alia* that in their dealings with the public Researchers must collect, process and use all personal data "fairly and lawfully"; be transparent in their explanations to Respondents of how their personal data will be handled and used; not place undue burdens on Respondents; and apply adequate safeguards to ensure the security of any personal data they collect unless and until it is made impossible to identify the data subject (i.e., the Respondent) and the data have therefore ceased to be "personal data." The requirements of national legislation may vary from country to country but the undertaking of market researchers to safeguard the rights of Respondents must remain the same.

These issues are dealt with under the provisions of Rules 3 and 4 of the International Code. These Rules require that:

- A respondent's personal data may be used only for the purposes for which they were collected and to which the Respondent has agreed. Under no circumstances may they be used for any non-research purpose.

- Such personal data must never be disclosed to anyone outside the research organisation(s) responsible for the project (other than for the limited and fully-safeguarded exceptions for necessary research purposes referred to below under Rule 4); and in any case only to authorised personnel who need such access for the purposes of research.

While any data remain in personalised form strict security arrangements must be in place, and enforced, to prevent any unauthorised access to them.

Organisations carrying out marketing research must have the appropriate internal procedures and controls in place, and are advised to establish ISO 9001 or equivalent Standards, to ensure that legislative and other requirements are not contravened. Putting such controls in place is primarily the responsibility of those organisations. Individual Researchers subscribing to the ICC/ESOMAR International Code must however always ensure that their own conduct fully conforms to the principles summarised above and embodied in the Code's Rules.

(RULE 3)

When asking Respondents for their co-operation in a marketing research project they must be told:

1. The identity of the organisation or individual who is collecting the data (see also Rule 8).

2. The type(s) of person or organisation who will receive the results.

3. The general purposes for which the results will be used.

Respondents must also be informed, where it is not already obvious, that their co-operation in the project is entirely voluntary.

Where requested by the Respondent the latter must be told how their name came to be selected for interview. They must also be assured that any personal data they provide will be used for statistical research purposes only and will not result at any stage in any direct marketing approach being made to the individual Respondent.

Researchers and those working on their behalf (e.g., interviewers) must not, in order to secure the co-operation of Respondents or others, make statements or promises that they know or believe to be incorrect—for example about the likely length of the interview or about the possibilities of being re-interviewed on a later occasion. In addition, any assurances given to Respondents must be fully honoured.

Where it is possible that the Researcher might wish to re-contact the Respondent for a further interview at a later date (for example in the case of a longitudinal research project) permission for this must be obtained from the Respondent not later than the end of the first interview except in the rare cases where there is some valid methodological reason to the contrary.

A Respondent is entitled to withdraw from an interview or research project at any stage and to refuse to cooperate in it further. Any or all of the information collected from the Respondent must be destroyed without unreasonable delay if the Respondent so requests.

Where fieldwork is subcontracted the Researcher must ensure in the contract with the interviewers that the latter understand and fully conform to the requirements of Rule 3.

(RULE 4)

Before collecting or otherwise processing any personal data Researchers must ensure that, if required by law, they and/or their organisation are appropriately registered with the relevant national data protection authority.

Since data protection legislation applies only to "personal data" Researchers should wherever possible plan to "de-personalise" such data as soon as possible after collection and the completion of any necessary quality control checks on the data. Where for technical or other reasons this is not practicable then any data must be securely stored in a way which prevents any unauthorised access for any purpose other than one needed to meet the objectives of the research project.

As long as it remains possible to link particular individuals to their responses there must be adequate security arrangements in force to ensure that any personal data is not accessible, accidentally or otherwise, by unauthorised individuals either inside or outside the Researcher's organisation. Authorisation for such access must be given only on a "need-to-know" basis and exclusively for research purposes. Such security precautions are necessary for all types of personal data, especial care being essential with the security of any data which might be regarded as particularly sensitive for any reason.

Where—for example in the case of panel or other longitudinal research studies—it is technically necessary to maintain files of research data in a form where the identity of Respondents is (at least potentially) identifiable the existence of such a research database must be registered with the national data protection registrar whenever required by law. Taking into account the requirements of Rule 3, Researchers must ensure that:

- The Respondents involved have been adequately informed about, and agreed to, the nature of the research and the form of data processing involved.

- They understand that they can withdraw from the research at any stage before or after it has started.

- They have agreed to the maintenance of the necessary data file.

- They understand that they have the right at any stage of the research to know what personal data are held on them in the files, and that while these data are still held in personalised form they can ask for part or all of them to be corrected or destroyed, and that the Researcher must conform to any such requests whenever it is reasonable to do so.

- A security system is in place which at all times effectively prevents any unauthorized person from having access to any personal data provided by Respondents, and that the data are used exclusively for the purposes of scientific marketing research.

In any case where personal data are to be transferred between countries the Researcher must ensure that the level of data protection applied to the processing of personal data in the other countries involved is at least as high as that applying in the country where the data were originally collected. If there is any doubt about this the appropriate level of data protection to be applied must be specified in a written contract with the relevant parties in those other countries.

A Researcher must not disclose personal data to any person or body outside the research organisation(s) responsible for the project without the explicit permission of the Respondent for such disclosure in accordance with the requirements of Rule 4. In addition, one of the following two provisions must apply:

- The disclosure is exclusively for the purposes of research and not for any other purpose. (Where the disclosure of Respondents' names/identities is to a third party such as a subcontractor this must be essential for a research purpose such as data collection or analysis or further interview— for example, for an independent fieldwork quality control check.)
- Where Researchers co-operating in the same survey need to exchange Respondents' personal data in order to carry out different elements of the study—for example, in a combined quantitative and qualitative research study. In such a case Respondents must be told in advance that a different research agency may be contacting them for this purpose, and have agreed to this.

In all such cases the Researcher in overall charge of the project must ensure that all parties concerned agree to abide by the requirements of the ICC/ESOMAR International Code, as elaborated by these Notes, and by the requirements of relevant data protection legislation. If any parties have not already formally subscribed to the Code the Researcher must secure their agreement, in writing, to do so.

It should be noted that even these limited exceptions may not be permitted in certain countries. In such cases the Researcher must always comply with the national requirements on data protection.

(RULE 5)

The Researcher must explicitly agree with the Client arrangements regarding the responsibilities for product safety and for dealing with any complaints or damage arising from faulty products or product misuse. Such responsibilities will normally rest with the Client, but the Researcher must ensure that products are correctly stored and handled while in the Researcher's charge and that Respondents are given appropriate instructions for their use.

More generally, Researchers should avoid interviewing at inappropriate or inconvenient times. They should also avoid the use of unnecessarily long interviews; and the asking of personal questions that may worry or annoy Respondents, unless the information is essential to the purposes of the study and the reasons for needing it are explained to the Respondent.

(RULE 6)

The definitions of "children" and "young people" vary by country. If not otherwise specified locally, Researchers should assume that such references apply respectively to those "under 14 years" and between "14–17 years." This issue is addressed in detail in the ESOMAR Guideline on Interviewing Children and Young People.

(RULE 7)

The Respondent must be told at the beginning of the interview that recording techniques are to be used unless this knowledge might bias the Respondent's subsequent behaviour. In the latter category of cases, the Respondent must be told about the recording at the end of the interview and be given the opportunity to see or hear the relevant section of the record and, if he/she so wishes, to have this destroyed.

Researchers should note that tape and video recordings of interviews with Respondents constitute personal data for the purposes of the EU Data Protection Directive. Researchers carrying out research within the EU must therefore process information collected by such means in the same way as they would any other personal data they collect (i.e., fully in accordance with the provisions of the ICC/ESOMAR Code, as elaborated by these Notes).

A "public place" is one to which the public has free access and where an individual reasonably could expect to be observed and/or overheard by other people (*e.g.*, in a shop or on the street).

The more specific issues that arise with tape and video-recording of interviews are dealt with in the ESOMAR Guideline on this subject (N.B. The Guideline also deals with the situation where interviews are to be observed by a client).

(RULE 8)

The name and address/telephone number of the Company normally must be given to the Respondent at the time of interview.

In the case of subcontracted fieldwork the Respondent must be given the relevant details of the agency responsible for subcontracting the work.

In the case of research using the Internet the Respondent must be given an appropriate email address at which to contact the Researcher.

Whenever possible "Free phone" or similar facilities should be provided so that Respondents can check the Researcher's bona fides without cost to themselves.

C. The Professional Responsibilities of Researchers

Section C of the ICC/ESOMAR Code is not intended to restrict the rights of Researchers to undertake any legitimate marketing research activity and to operate competitively in so doing. However, it is essential that in pursuing these objectives the general public's confidence in the integrity of marketing research is not undermined in any way. Section C summarises the responsibilities of Researchers to the public at large as well as to the marketing research profession.

(RULE 13)

Researchers must ensure that appropriate security systems are in place to ensure that at all stages of a marketing research project they comply fully with the provisions of the ICC/ESOMAR Code, as elaborated by these Notes, insofar as these relate to the protection of personal data.

(RULE 14)

The kinds of technical information that should be made available on request include those listed in the Notes to Rule 25. The Researcher must not, however, disclose information that is confidential to the Client's business, nor need he disclose information relating to parts of the survey that were not published.

(RULE 15)

The kinds of "non-research activity" that must not be associated in any way with the carrying out of marketing research include:

- Enquiries whose objectives are to obtain personal information about private individuals per se, whether for legal, political, supervisory (e.g., job performance), private or other purposes;
- The acquisition of information for use for credit-rating or similar purposes;
- The compilation, updating or enhancement of lists, registers or databases that are not for scientific research purposes (e.g., those that may be used for direct marketing);
- Industrial, commercial or any other form of espionage;

- Sales or promotional approaches to individual Respondents;
- The collection of debts; and
- Fund-raising.

Certain of these activities—in particular, the collection of information for databases for subsequent use in direct marketing and similar operations—are legitimate activities in their own right. Researchers (e.g., those working within a client company) may be involved with such activities either directly or indirectly. In such cases it is essential that a very clear distinction be made between such activities and marketing research. Any work that involves the collection and use of personal data for non-research purposes (such as those listed above) must not be carried out under the name of marketing research or of a marketing research organisation as such, or be *incorporated into* a marketing research survey. Personal data collected for marketing research purposes must *never* be used in connection with non-research activities such as direct marketing.

However, the use of marketing research data in connection with non-research databases is permissible where Researchers have first ensured that such research information has been fully depersonalised (i.e., anonymised). A common way of achieving this is by "modelling" the research data before its fusion with any other data. This is permissible only if there is no risk that any data in the database which is derived from marketing research could be linked to individual Respondents or Data Subjects.

These issues are considered at greater length in the ESOMAR Guideline on Maintaining the Distinctions between Marketing Research and Direct Marketing.

There are no additional requirements which apply to customer satisfaction research in cases where no personal data are disclosed outside the research organisation(s) responsible for the project. Furthermore, if a survey sample or mailing list has been provided for the project by an outside company (e.g., client or other research organisation) it is also reasonable for the Researcher to notify that company of any names and addresses which have been found during the course of the survey to be no longer operational (e.g., because a Respondent has died or moved away from the address given). The situation is more complex in the case of a study which may involve other data about identified Respondents (e.g., specific queries or comments) being disclosed outside the research organisation: these issues are addressed in more detail in a separate ESOMAR Guideline on Customer Satisfaction Research.

D. The Mutual Rights and Responsibilities of Researchers and Clients

Code Section D is not intended to regulate the details of business relationships between Researchers and Clients except insofar as involving principles of general interest and concern. Most such matters should be regulated by individual business contracts. It is clearly vital that such contracts be based on an adequate understanding and consideration of the issues involved: the ESOMAR Guidelines on Selecting a Marketing Research Agency and Reaching Agreement on a Marketing Research Project address these issues.

(RULE 17)

The ban on disclosing the identity of "other" clients does **not** apply when such disclosure has been previously agreed with those clients (e.g., in the case of certain jointly-sponsored "industry" surveys).

(RULE 18)

The Researcher must ensure that, wherever the use of any subcontractor may result in personal data being disclosed to that subcontractor, the latter will fully comply with all relevant data protection and related requirements as summarised in the Notes on Rule 4 above.

Although it is usually known in advance which subcontractors will be used, occasions do arise during the course of a project where subcontractors need to be brought in, or changed, at very short notice. In such cases, rather than cause delays to the project in order to inform the Client, it will usually be sensible and acceptable to let the Client know as quickly as possible after the decision has been taken.

(RULE 20)

This Rule does not prevent the Researcher from discussing relevant sections of the Client's research brief with an actual or potential subcontractor of that Researcher when this is necessary for the purposes of the research project. In such a case the Researcher is, of course, responsible for ensuring that the subcontractor fully conforms to this and other requirements of the Code.

(RULE 21)

Research proposals, research designs and questionnaires are, under the Berne Convention, the property of the Researcher by whom they were originally designed provided that:

- The material can be shown to be an original creation;

- The originator has explicitly laid claim in the appropriate way (in written form) to the copyright and can if required produce the necessary evidence of this; and

- The copyright has not been transferred to another party (e.g., a Client) by agreement between the parties involved.

The extent of protection in practice may to some extent depend upon the nature of the material and the interpretation of the law in different countries. However, whether or not plagiarism in a particular case is shown to have actually broken the law, it may well be unethical, and any serious example would be regarded as prima facie one of unprofessional conduct.

(RULE 22)

The proposed period of time for which research records should be kept by the Researcher will vary with the nature of the data (*e.g.*, whether they are personal or non-personal), the nature of the project (*e.g.*, ad hoc, panel, repetitive) and the possible requirements for follow-up research or further analysis.

The Researcher should take suitable precautions to guard against any accidental loss of the information, whether stored physically or electronically, during the agreed storage period.

Researchers must not retain personal data for longer than is necessary for the purposes of the specific study. With respect to the retention of personal data, Researchers must ensure compliance with all relevant data protection legislation and the requirements of the ICC/ESOMAR Code, especially Rule 4, as elaborated in these Notes.

In the case of non-personal data, the period of time for which records should be kept normally will be longer for the stored research data resulting from a survey (tabulations, discs, tapes, etc.) than for primary field records (the original completed questionnaires and similar basic records). The precise format in which records are stored is normally less important than the basic requirement that (unless previously agreed to the contrary and except to the extent that the reconstruction may result in the records becoming personalised) it should be possible to "reconstruct" all the information originally collected. The period of storage must be disclosed to, and agreed by, the Client in advance.

In default of any agreement to the contrary, in the case of ad hoc surveys the normal period for which the **primary field records** should be retained is one year after completion of the fieldwork while the **research data** should be stored for possible further analysis for at least two years.

(RULE 24)

On request, the client—or his mutually acceptable representative—may observe a limited number of interviews for this purpose. When this occurs the Researcher must first obtain the agreement of the Respondent concerned. In addition, any such observer must previously have agreed to comply with the provisions of the ICC/ESOMAR Code, especially Rule 4, as elaborated by these Notes. This agreement must be obtained in writing in any case where the observer has not already done this.

The Researcher is entitled to be recompensed for any delays and increased fieldwork costs that may result from such a request. The Client must be informed if the observation of interviews may mean that the results of such interviews will need to be excluded from the overall survey analysis because they are no longer methodologically comparable.

In the case of multi-client studies, the Researcher may require that any such observer is independent of any of the Clients.

Where an independent check on the quality of field-work is to be carried out by a different research agency the latter must conform in all respects to the provisions of the ICC/ESOMAR Code, as elaborated by these Notes. An agreement in writing to this effect must be obtained from that agency in any case where it has not already so agreed. If the third party agency has been instructed by the Client, and not by the Researcher, the Researcher must ensure that the Client enters into such an agreement with the third party agency. In particular, the anonymity of the original Respondents must be fully safeguarded and their names and addresses may be used exclusively for the purposes of backchecks, not being disclosed to the Client. Similar considerations apply where the Client wishes to carry out checks on the quality of data preparation work.

(RULE 25)

The Client is entitled to the following information about any marketing research project to which he has subscribed:

(1) Background
- For whom the study was conducted
- The purpose of the study
- Names of subcontractors and consultants performing any substantial part of the work

(2) Sample
- A description of the intended and actual universe covered

- The size, nature and geographical distribution of the sample (both planned and achieved); and where relevant, the extent to which any of the data collected were obtained from only part of the sample
- Details of the sampling method and any weighting methods used
- When technically relevant, a statement of response rates and a discussion of any possible bias due to non-response

(3) Data collection
- A description of the method by which the information was collected
- A description of the field staff, briefing and field quality control methods used
- The method of recruiting Respondents; and the general nature of any incentives offered to secure their cooperation
- When the fieldwork was carried out
- In the case of "desk research", a clear statement of the sources of the information and their likely reliability

(4) Presentation of results
- The relevant factual findings obtained
- Bases of percentages (both weighted and unweighted)
- General indicators of the probable statistical margins of error to be attached to the main findings, and of the levels of statistical significance of differences between key figures

- The questionnaire and other relevant documents and materials used (or, in the case of a shared project, that portion relating to the matter reported on).

The report on a project normally should cover the above points or provide a reference to a readily available separate document containing the information.

(RULE 27)

It is clearly impossible for a Researcher fully to control the ways in which research findings are interpreted or applied once these are in the public domain. However, Researchers should use their best endeavours to prevent any misinterpretation or misuse of research findings, and (as far as is practicable) to correct any such misinterpretation or misuse once they become aware that this has happened.

The publication of research findings may sometimes prove to be misleading because certain of the technical aspects or limitations of the research have not been fully appreciated and/or because the public presentation, explanation and discussion of the findings (e.g., in the media) have not clearly spelt out all the relevant considerations. This can happen accidentally, or as a result of the pressures on media time and space, rather than for any more undesirable reason.

Researchers can reduce the danger of such problems arising by making sure (e.g., in their contract for a research project) that they are consulted in advance by the Client about the form in which any research findings will be published. If following publication it becomes clear that serious misinterpretation of the research and its findings has occurred, leading to misleading discussion of the implications of the research, the Researcher should endeavour to correct such misinterpretation by any available and appropriate means.

In a case where the Client does not consult and agree in advance the form of publication with the Researcher, the latter is entitled to:

(i) refuse permission for his name to be used in connection with the published findings and

(ii) publish the appropriate technical details of the project (as listed in the Notes to Rule 25).

(RULE 29)

It is recommended that Researchers specify in their research proposals that they follow the requirements of the ICC/ESOMAR Code and that they make a copy available to the Client if the latter does not already have one.

Section E. Implementation of the Code

The addresses to which queries, or reports of possible Code infringements, should be sent are those on the inside front cover of the Code itself. Any such communications should be marked "For the attention of":

- The Professional Standards Committee, ESOMAR, Vondelstraat 172, 1054 GV Amsterdam, The Netherlands

- The International Secretariat, ICC, 38 Cours Albert 1er, 75008 Paris, France

Possible infringements of the ICC/ESOMAR Code by members of ESOMAR will be investigated initially by the Society's Professional Standards Committee, which has powers to warn or reprimand offenders. If after initial investigation the case appears to be one that might call for more severe sanctions, it will be referred to ESOMAR's Disciplinary Committee. This Committee, under an independent Chairman, has the powers to suspend or expel members found guilty, after further investigation, of any serious contravention of the Code. When appropriate the relevant authorities also will be notified (*e.g.*, the National Data Protection Authority in the case of an infringement of data protection legislation).

The detailed disciplinary procedures are set out in the ESOMAR publication entitled "ESOMAR Disciplinary Procedures".

For a research agency to be eligible to be listed in the ESOMAR Directory, its chief executive officer must have signed an undertaking that the company will conform in all respects to the requirements of the ICC/ESOMAR Code, as elaborated by these Notes. Any breach of this undertaking may lead to the withdrawal of the Directory listing.

References

How to Commission Research, including:
- Selecting a Marketing Research Agency

- Reaching Agreement on a Marketing Research Project
- International Research

Mystery Shopping

Interviewing Children and Young People

Maintaining the Distinctions between Marketing Research and Direct Marketing

Customer Satisfaction Research (in preparation)

Tape and Video-recording of Interviews and Group Discussions

ESOMAR Guideline on Pharmaceutical Marketing Research

Internet Privacy Policies and Privacy Statements

Also relevant:

The ESOMAR/WAPOR Guide to Opinion Polls, including ESOMAR International Code of Practice for the Publication of Public Opinion Polls Results

ESOMAR Guideline on Pharmaceutical Marketing Research

ESOMAR/ARF Guideline on Conducting Marketing and Opinion Research using the Internet

Annexe to Notes

EUROPEAN DATA PROTECTION REQUIREMENTS

Introduction

Rule 2 of the ICC/ESOMAR International Code of Marketing and Social Research Practice ("ICC/ESOMAR Code" or "Code") requires compliance with any and all national and international legal requirements affecting marketing research. This Annexe summarises requirements within the European Union ("EU") relating to the collection and handling of personal data.

The base measure discussed in this Annexe is EU Directive 95/46/EC "on the protection of individuals with regard to the processing of personal data and on the free movement of such data" ("EU Data Protection Directive" or "Directive"). As approved by the European Parliament and Council, the EU Data Protection Directive requires EU Member States to enact conforming laws, regulations and administrative provisions and to enforce such measures in the manner described in the Directive.

Researchers operating within the EU should familiarise themselves with the provisions of the EU Data Protection Directive. But that alone is not sufficient. They also should review, and must comply with, national data protection requirements in the various EU Member States, at least those in which they are operating. The reason is that such requirements are not entirely uniform: and also that their interpretation may in certain cases depend on how they are applied in practice in the individual countries.

This annexe is designed to familiarise researchers with the core data protection principles established by the EU Data Protection Directive. Country-specific data protection requirements are not identified in the discussion that follows.

When carrying out research within the EU Researchers will therefore need to ensure that they have set up and follow appropriate operating procedures which conform to the requirements of the Articles summarised below.

Purposes

Article 1 of the EU Data Protection Directive requires Member States to "protect the fundamental rights and freedoms of natural persons, and in particular their right to privacy with respect to the processing of personal data." In pursuing that objective, the Directive instructs Member States that they should "neither restrict nor prohibit the free flow of personal data between Member States" in an unnecessary or inappropriate manner.

Definitions

Article 2 of the EU Data Protection Directive sets forth the following definitions, which also appear in most Member State data protection measures:

Consent—the freely given and informed agreement by a person (i.e., the "data subject") to the processing of his/her personal data. The data subject may withdraw his/her consent at any time and may attach any condition or limitation he/she believes to be appropriate.

Controller—the individual or undertaking (e.g., the Researcher or research agency) that determines (alone or jointly with others) the purposes for which, and the manner in which, personal data are or will be processed.

Personal Data—any information relating to an identified or identifiable natural person (i.e., a private individual as opposed to a corporate or other comparable entity). An identifiable person is someone who can be identified, directly or indirectly, in particular by reference to an identification number or the person's physical, physiological, mental, economic, cultural or social characteristics.

Personal Data Filing System any set of personal data which is structured, either by reference to individuals or by reference to criteria relating to individuals, in such a way that specific information relating to a particular individual is readily accessible. This includes both automated and manual records, whether they are centralised, decentralised or dispersed on a functional or geographical basis.

Processing of Personal Data—includes, but is not limited to, their collection, recording, organisation, storage, adaptation or alteration, retrieval, consultation, use, disclosure by transmission, dissemination or otherwise making available, alignment or combination, blocking, erasure or destruction, whether by automated means or otherwise.

National Laws

Article 4 of the EU Data Protection Directive provides guidance to controllers in deciding which national law applies to any data processing activities for which they have responsibility. It generally instructs controllers to comply with the law of the Member State in which the controller is established (i.e., is located) and in which processing is carried out. When the controller is responsible for, and/or established in, several Member States he must ensure that he complies with the laws of all these Member States in which data processing is taking place. (These requirements cover all aspects of data processing, as defined above, including the use of processing equipment except where the latter is used solely for the purpose of transferring data through the territory of the Community).

If the controller on a particular project has not been established in any country within the EU, the controller must designate a representative who is so established. Article 4 provides, however, that any such arrangement is "without prejudice to legal actions [that] could be initiated against the controller himself."

Data Quality

Article 6 establishes certain principles relating to "data quality." These state that personal data must be:

- Processed fairly and lawfully;
- Collected for specific, explicit and legitimate purposes and not "further processed" in a way incompatible with those purposes (NB: The Directive provides that the "further processing" of data for historical, statistical or scientific purposes is not to be deemed to be incompatible with the initial purpose(s) provided appropriate safeguards have been provided by the particular Member State(s).);

- Adequate, relevant and not excessive in relation to the purposes for which they are to be collected and/or are to be further processed;

- Accurate and, when necessary, kept up to date, with every reasonable step being taken to ensure that data that are inaccurate or incomplete, having regard to the purpose(s) for which they were collected or for which they are being further processed, are erased or rectified; and

- Kept in a form that permits data subjects to be identified for no longer than is necessary (NB: Member States are required to establish safeguards for personal data stored for longer periods for historical, statistical or scientific purposes).

Other Limits on Data Processing

Article 7 establishes certain additional criteria for the processing of personal data. In most cases, personal data may be processed only if "the data subject has unambiguously given his consent." There are certain exceptions to this requirement but in general they are unlikely to apply to most marketing research work. Without the data subject's consent, personal data may be processed only if needed to:

- Perform a contract to which the data subject is a party or take steps at the request of the data subject prior to entering into a contract;

- Comply with a legal obligation to which the data controller is subject;

- Protect the vital interests of the data subject;

- Perform a task carried out in the public interest or in the exercise of official authority vested in the controller or a third party to whom the data are to be or have been disclosed; or

- Serve other legitimate purposes, "except where such interests are overridden by the . . . fundamental rights and freedoms of the data subject. . . ."

The processing of personal data falling within the last two categories (i.e., the "public interest/official authority" and "other legitimate purposes" categories) must be stopped if the data subject informs the data controller of a "justified objection."

Special Categories of Data

Article 8 defines such data as "personal data revealing racial or ethnic origin, political opinions, religious or philosophical beliefs, trade-union membership, and the processing of data concerning health or sex life." The processing of such data is prohibited unless one or more of the exceptions specified in the Directive have been met. The most important of these exceptions, in the case of marketing research, is the first—namely where "the data subject has given his explicit consent to the processing of such data" (except in a case where national law prohibits the giving of such consent).

The remaining exceptions are in most cases less relevant to most marketing research and cover situations where:

- The data subject has given his/her explicit consent, except where national law prohibits the giving of consent;

- The processing is required to satisfy the obligations of the data controller in the field of national employment law and national law imposes "adequate safeguards";

- The processing is needed to protect the vital interests of the data subject or another person and the data subject is physically or legally incapable of giving consent;

- The processing will be carried out in a controlled and otherwise appropriate manner by a foundation, association or other non-profit body with a political, philosophical, religious or trade-union aim "and on condition that the processing relates solely to the members of the body or to persons who have regular contact with it in connection with its purposes and the data are not disclosed to a third party without the consent of the data subjects"; or

- The processing relates to data that have "manifestly [been] made public by the data subject or is necessary for the establishment, exercise or defence of legal claims."

Article 8 establishes a special, although carefully defined and limited, exception for health-related information. According to subsection 3 of Article 8, health-related data may be processed—even without the data subject's consent—when "required for the purposes of preventative medicine, medical diagnosis, the provision of care or treatment or the management of health-care services, and where those data are processed by a health professional subject under national law or rules established by competent bodies to the obligation of professional secrecy or by another person also subject to an equivalent obligation of secrecy."

In the case of scientific Marketing Research which conforms to the data protection requirements of the ICC/ESOMAR Code the handling of special categories of data need not in general pose special problems, but it is essential that Researchers ensure that all their procedures are fully in accordance with the relevant Rules and legislation when dealing with such data.

Information to Be Given to the Data Subject

Article 10 specifies that, when data are obtained directly from a data subject, the controller or the controller's representative must inform the data subject of:

- The identity of the controller and of the controller's representative, if any;

- The purpose(s) for which the data are being collected and will be processed; and

- Any further information the data subject may need to guarantee fair processing of the data— such as the types of person or organisation that will receive the data, the voluntary nature (or otherwise) of the data subject's participation, and the data subject's right to access and correct data concerning him/her.

While Article 11 imposes broadly similar requirements when the data are not obtained directly from the data subject, such requirements do not apply in the case of "processing for statistical purposes or for the purposes of statistical or scientific research" and where "the provision of such information proves impossible or would involve a disproportionate effort."

Other Data Subject Rights

Article 12 confers upon data subjects the right to obtain from the data controller "without constraint at reasonable intervals and without excessive delay and expense" the following:

- Confirmation concerning whether the controller is holding or otherwise processing personal data relating to him/her;

- Information on the purpose(s) of the processing, the categories of data concerned, and the recipients or categories of recipients;

- Information "in an intelligible form" concerning the data relating to him/her being processed and the source of such data; and

- Information, in certain circumstances, concerning the "logic" underlying any automated data processing (this requirement however applies primarily to activities other than statistical and scientific marketing research).

Article 12 also gives data subjects the right to require "as appropriate" the "rectification, erasure or blocking of data" whenever the processing of such data does not comply with the provisions of the EU Data Protection Directive, "in particular because of the incomplete or inaccurate nature of the data." If data have been corrected or are subject to erasure or blocking, the controller must alert any third parties to whom the data have been disclosed of the action that was taken, unless such notification "proves impossible or involves a disproportionate effort."

However, Article 13 allows certain exemptions to the requirements of Article 12. Importantly it specifies that Member States may dispense with those requirements in cases which are "subject to adequate legal safeguards, in particular that the data are not used for taking measures or decisions regarding any particular individual, " where "there is clearly no risk of breaching the privacy of the data subject", and when "data are processed solely for the purposes of scientific research or are kept in personal form for a period which does not exceed the period necessary for the sole purpose of creating statistics."

Article 14 confers upon data subjects the right to object, "on request and free of charge, to the processing of personal data relating to him[/her] [that] the controller anticipates being processed for the purposes of direct marketing." That includes the right to be informed in advance—that is, before personal data are disclosed for marketing purposes to a third party "for the first time."

Confidentiality and Security

Articles 16 and 17 impose confidentiality and security safeguards. Most fundamentally, data controllers are required to take appropriate steps, including steps of a technical and organisational nature, to protect personal data from accidental or unlawful destruction or accidental loss, alteration or disclosure. Controllers also must enter into a **written** agreement with any subcontractor who is to process data on the controller's behalf, confirming the subcontractor's agreement to process personal data in accordance with the controller's instructions and to implement technical and organisational measures equivalent to those required of the controller.

Notification of National Data Protection Authorities

Article 18 instructs Member States to require the controller or his representative, if any, to register with the data protection authority before collecting or otherwise processing personal data. Member States may, where they so decide, allow registration on a generic basis with a general—non-project-specific—filing being made by the controller, especially for "categories of processing operations which are unlikely, taking into account of the data to be processed, to affect adversely the rights and freedoms of data subjects."

Whenever advance notification of a project is required, this must, according to Article 19, include at least the following information:

- The name and address of the controller and of his/her personal representative, if any;
- The purpose(s) of the processing;

- A description of the category or categories of data subject and of the data or categories of data relating to them;

- The recipients or categories of recipients to whom the data might be disclosed;

- Proposed transfers of data to third countries (*i.e.,* countries other than those within the European Economic Area, which consists of the EU Member States plus Iceland, Liechtenstein and Norway); and

- A general description permitting a preliminary assessment to be made of the appropriateness of the measures that will be taken to ensure the security of data processing.

International Transfers of Personal Data

Article 25 generally prohibits the transfer of personal data to any country outside the European Economic Area unless such country "ensures an adequate level of protection." Judgements concerning adequacy are supposed to take into account a variety of factors, including the nature of the data, the purpose and duration of the proposed processing operations, the country of data origin and destination, and the legal requirements and professional standards observed in the particular country. If adequate safeguards have not been implemented in the third country, a national data protection authority nonetheless may authorise the transfer if convinced that the contract pursuant to which the transfer is to be made requires the recipient to afford an adequate level of security.

Article 26 exempts from the foregoing the following transfers of personal data to non-European Economic Area countries:

- Transfers to which the data subject has given his/her unambiguous consent (this would include knowledge of the country and entity to which their personal data might be transferred);

- Transfers that are needed for the performance of a contract between the data subject and the controller or to implement a pre-contractual commitment made at the request of the data subject;

- Transfers that are needed for the conclusion or performance of a contract concluded in the interest of the data subject between the controller and a third party;

- Transfers that are needed or are legally required on important public interest grounds or for the establishment, exercise or defence of legal claims;

- Transfers that are needed to protect the vital interests of the data subject; and

- Transfers that are made from a register established pursuant to laws and regulations as being opcn for consultation by members of the general public or by any person who can demonstrate a legitimate interest.

Sector-Specific Codes of Conduct

Article 27 instructs the EU Commission and Member States to encourage the drawing up of codes of conduct "intended to contribute to the proper implementation of the national provisions adopted by the Member States pursuant to [the EU Data Protection] Directive, taking account of the specific features of the various sectors." Provision has been made for the submission of such codes to the pertinent national data protection authorities and the Working Party created by Article 29 of the EU Data Protection Directive.

Remedies, Liability and Sanctions

Article 22 through 24 confer upon the individual EU Member States responsibility for adopting "suitable" measures, including specific sanctions, ensuring full implementation of the EU Data Protection Directive. According to Article 22, Member State enforcement measures must include, at a minimum, recognition of "the right of every person to a judicial remedy for any breach of the rights guaranteed . . . by the national law applicable to the [data] processing in question." Member States also must ensure that anyone damaged by an act incompatible with applicable data protection guarantees may "receive compensation from the controller for the damage suffered.

277

ICC/ESOMAR International Code

The core requirements of the EU Data Protection Directive, insofar as they concern marketing research, have
been reflected in the ICC/ESOMAR Code since the Code
was first formulated over 50 years ago. Those of the Directive's requirements, summarised above, which affect
the carrying out of marketing research are taken into account in the Notes to the ICC/ESOMAR International
Code.

It is important to emphasise that once data have been
de-personalised, so that they no longer can be linked to
any natural person, they do not constitute "personal data"
as defined in the EU Data Protection Directive. The right
that data subjects otherwise would have to access and
otherwise control or object to data processing expires at
such time. The ICC/ESOMAR Code and accompanying
Notes incorporate the same limitation, which is based on
acknowledgement that the privacy interests of data subjects cannot be compromised by the disclosure of data
that can be linked to any individual.

Any self-regulatory code implementing the EU Data
Protection Directive and/or related national laws must be
accompanied by appropriate disciplinary procedures and
sanctions. These are referred to in Section E of the
ICC/ESOMAR Code and the accompanying Notes on this.
A full description of the procedures to be utilised and the
sanctions that may be imposed in the event of a violation
of the ICC/ESOMAR Code, including the provisions

dealing with the processing of personal data, is contained in a separate ESOMAR publication entitled "ESOMAR Disciplinary Procedures."

ICC

International Chamber of Commerce

38 Cours Albert 1er

5008 Paris

France

Tel: +33-1-4953.2828

Fax: +33-1-4953.2859

Email: icc@iccwbo.org

Web site: *www.iccwbo.org*

Appendix 3
International Research
Associations

**Alliance of International Market Research Institutes
(AIMRI)**
26 Granard Avenue
London SW15 6HJ UK
Tel: +44 20 878 03343
www.aimri.org

American Marketing Association (AMA)
311 S. Wacker Drive, Suite 5800
Chicago, IL 60606 USA
Tel: 800-AMA-1150
www.marketingpower.com

British Market Research Association
Secretariat, Devonshire House, 60 Goswell Road
London EC1M 7AD UK
Tel: +44 20 7566 3636
www.bmra.org.uk

Canadian Association of Marketing Research Associations (CAMRO)
6835 Century Avenue, Second Floor
Mississauga, ON L5N 2L2 Canada
Tel: 905-826-5437
www.camro.org

Council of American Survey Research Organizations (CASRO)
170 North Country Road, Suite 4
Port Jefferson, NY 11777 USA
Tel: 516-928-6954
www.casro.org

European Society for Opinion and Marketing Research (ESOMAR)
Central Secretariat, Vondelstraat 172
1054 GV Amsterdam, The Netherlands
Tel: +31 20 664 2141
www.esomar.org

Japan Marketing Research Association
No. 1 Magami Building, 1-5
Koraku 1-chome, Bunkyo-ku
Tokyo, 112-0004 Japan
Tel: +81 2 2813 3577
www.jmra-net.or.jp

Market Research Society (MRS)
15 Northburgh Street
London EC1V OJR UK
Tel: +44 20 7490 4911
www.mrs.org.uk

Marketing Research Association (MRA)
110 National Drive, 2nd Floor
Glastonberry, CT 06033 USA
Tel: 860-682-1000
www.mra-net.org

Qualitative Research Consultants Association (QRCA)
380 East Cumberland Road, P.O. Box 967
Camden, TN 38320 USA
Tel: 731-584-8080
www.qrca.org

Appendix 4
Case Study

This case study ties together a number of the topics covered in this book. It begins with a Request for Proposal (RFP) issued by a client, followed by a resulting market research vendor's proposal for the project and concluding with a top-line report of the results of the study. All companies, managers, study objectives and resulting data are entirely fictional and should only be considered in terms of how these documents might appear in a research situation.

Also note that a top-line report, similar to what is provided in this case study, is typically an initial "glance" at the data generally followed by a detailed executive summary report shortly thereafter. Given the fictional nature of this report, it is somewhat leaner than you might expect to receive from your research supplier.

Example A

REQUEST FOR PROPOSAL
PREMIER PCS INTERNATIONAL
PURCHASE PROCESS STUDY

1. Introduction

Premier PCs International (PPCI) is seeking proposals for a follow-up study of business desktop and laptop computer purchasers. The initial study was conducted approximately one year ago and PPCI wants to assess changes in its marketplace.

2. Objectives

PPCI's research objectives are as follows:

- Analysis of the steps and decisions a purchaser follows when selecting a business desktop or laptop.
- Identification of key selection and purchase criteria.
- Identification of primary information sources that business customers use in making their purchase decision.
- Evaluation of customers' consideration of warranties at time of purchase.
- Identification of preferred channels for business customers purchasing desktop and/or laptop computers.

3. Target Respondents

The study will be conducted with primary business purchase decision-makers for desktop and/or laptop computers. Their decision must include the brand selection. Business sizes are as follows:

- Micro (1–10 employees)
- Small (11–100 employees)
- Medium (101–1,000 employees)
- Large (1,001–9,999 employees)
- Corporate/Enterprise (10,000 or more employees)

4. Methodology

The research is to be conducted via telephone in the US, UK and Australia using a similar questionnaire as was used in the initial version of this study.

5. Reporting

The selected research supplier will provide PPCI with the following at the completion of the survey:

- A summary report including findings and, as applicable, recommendations
- Data tables
- An in-person presentation to management

6. Schedule

Immediately upon selection of the research supplier, PPCI will schedule an initial meeting/briefing with the supplier's project team. From that point it is expected that the study will be completed within one month. Please provide a timeline which includes your estimated schedule by task.

7. Proposal Format

Responses to this RFP should include names of key supplier team members, a timeline, estimated costs broken out by phase of the study and a detailed sample plan. PPCI will consider recommendations related to variations on our proposed methodology, etc., but please be specific in your proposal.

The proposal should be delivered electronically to the attention of Pat Smith at *p.smith@ppci.com* no later than 5:00 PM on July 16, 20XX. Any questions related to this RFP should also be addressed to Pat.

Example B
PURCHASE PROCESS STUDY
PROPOSAL FOR:
PREMIER PCS INTERNATIONAL
PRESENTED BY:
ABC RESEARCH & CONSULTING

1. Background Information

Premier PCs International (PPCI) develops and markets a range of desktop and laptop computers to business users in a number of countries around the globe. PPCI commissioned ABC Research & Consulting (ABC) one year ago to conduct a large-scale research study with the objective of developing a thorough understanding of the purchase decision process for its various desktop and laptop products within different segments of business customers ranging from micro-businesses to corporate enterprises.

This study was conducted in the United States, the United Kingdom and Australia, still its three key markets. The study was designed using a step-by-step process and procedure analysis method, based on a single recent purchase of a business desktop or laptop computer. This design allowed ABC to highlight specifically when during the purchase process business customers make their decisions related to brand and model as well as what sources of information influence their decisions. The main purpose of the original study was to determine what PPCI has to do, when they have to do it and in what way they need to do it in order to influence these customers to choose PPCI's products. Success in this area should then drive increased revenues as well as business customer loyalty.

2. Research Objectives

The objectives of the initial study remain similar in the proposed follow-up wave:

- Analyze the steps and decisions a purchaser follows in order to select a business desktop or laptop (from initial decision that the product is required to the actual purchase of a specific product to meet the business need).

- Identify the key selection and purchase criteria involved in the purchase decision and determine what role each of these criteria plays in the actual decision process.
- Determine what various types of information and information sources business customers use to select a product and to evaluate PPCI's products against those offered by the competition.
- Evaluate the extent to which customers consider/purchase services (i.e., warranties, etc.) at the time they make their desktop or laptop computer purchase.
- Identify the channels used by business customers when they purchase desktop and laptop computers.

In order to be consistent with the prior study, ABC will attempt to keep as much of the original questionnaire as possible intact in this version. This will allow comparisons between the two waves of data, thereby permitting PPCI to track any changes in customer behavior.

3. Research Methodology
Target Audience
The target audience for this survey will consist of firms in each of the following business size categories defined by number of employees:

- Micro-Businesses (1–10 employees)
- Small Businesses (11–100 employees)
- Medium Businesses (101–1000 employees)
- Large Businesses (1,001–9,999 employees)
- Corporate/Enterprise Businesses (10,000+ employees)

Within each of these categories, respondents will qualify by being the primary purchase decision-maker for desktop and/or laptop business computers. Their decision responsibilities must include the brand decision for these products.

In micro-business firms, decision-makers can also be the end users of the products purchased. It is recognized, however, that in the large and corporate/enterprise businesses there may be multiple purchase decision-makers sharing in the purchase decision process. For example, larger companies may have preferred or recommended brand lists for purchasers to select from. In these situations, respondents will be considered qualified if they are either identified as making the decision or as providing significant input to the specific desktop or laptop computer to be purchased. These respondents are likely to include end-users, department managers and IT professionals.

As in the initial wave, this research study will consist of interviews with qualified decision-makers who have purchased a qualifying desktop or laptop computer during the last six months. The study will be conducted, as in Wave 1, in PPCI's key markets of the United States, the United Kingdom and Australia.

Data Collection Method
Wave 1 of the PPCI study was conducted primarily via telephone interviews. ABC has, however, determined that its e-panel specifications will allow detailed profiling within the required business segments. This will allow ABC to conduct Wave 2 of the study via Web survey while maintaining the integrity of the question wording throughout the interview.

Sample Size and Design
The following sample plan is recommended for the proposed research study:

Business Size	Quota			
	US	UK	Australia	Totals
Micro	100	100	100	**300**
Small	100	100	100	**300**
Medium	100	100	100	**300**
Large	100	100	100	**300**
Corporate/Enterprise	100	100	100	**300**
Totals:	**500**	**500**	**500**	**1500**

In addition, there will be a quota within each category of 60% desktop purchasers and 40% laptop purchasers. At least one-third of respondents will be screened as PPCI customers.

4. Research Analysis & Reporting
ABC will provide Wave 2 reporting based on the analytical model and the presentation plan developed for Wave1. This will, however, be aug-

mented to analyze changes in customer purchase decision-making, brand preferences, etc. in comparison to Wave 1.

The following deliverables will be provided to PPCI upon completion of the survey:

- Initial top-line report highlighting key findings.
- Executive summary report providing key findings and recommendations based on the survey results.
- Product category reports.
- Data file with banner points to allow for additional analysis as required.
- Formal in-person presentation to PPCI management (date to be determined).

5. Logistics

Project Management

The project will be conducted under the immediate management of Rebecca James. Ms. James will be responsible for the overall quality of the research project and the related deliverables for the study. Edmund Davis will be be responsible for the day-to-day management of the research study as well as formulating the presentation and final reports, conclusions and recommendations.

Briefing & Quality Control

Teleconference kick-off meeting with PPCI to confirm that the team is all on "the same page" re: the project objectives and project plans:

- PPCI will have final approval authority for the survey instrument prior to programming the Web survey.
- A formal, detailed debriefing session with the project team (PPCI and ABC) to discuss results, conclusions and recommendations prior to final reporting and presentation.

6. Timeframe

The overall timeframe for the proposed project is as follows based on the associated research tasks:

- Kick-off meeting/initial questionnaire   5 days
- Client approval of questionnaire/survey programming   5 days
- Data collection   10 days
- Data processing   4 days
- Reporting/presentation preparations   10 days

7. Research Budget

ABC Research & Consulting's estimated costs for the project as defined in the preceding sections of this proposal is as follows (in US dollars):

- Project Design/Management $ 12,500
- Web Survey Programming/Sampling/Hosting   150,000
- Analysis/Reporting/Presentation   28,500
- Miscellaneous Expenses   1,500
- Total Estimated Costs: $192,500

Invoices are payable at 50% upon commission and 50% following the presentation. The preceding estimate includes all three countries and can be broken down by country if required.

Example C

BUSINESS PURCHASE PROCESS STUDY
TOP-LINE SUMMARY REPORT
PREPARED FOR: PREMIER PCS INTERNATIONAL
PREPARED BY: ABC RESEARCH & CONSULTING

CONTENTS

- Background, Objectives & Methodology
- Purchase Process Summary
- Resources Used in Purchase Decision
- Channels for Purchasing

BACKGROUND, OBJECTIVES & METHODOLOGY

Background

This research was conducted with the purpose of enabling PPCI to develop a detailed understanding of the purchase decision processes facing its business customers.

Objectives

Specific research objectives are to:

- Analyze the steps and decisions a purchaser follows in order to select a business desktop or laptop (from initial decision that the product is required to the actual purchase of a specific product to meet the business need).
- Identify the key selection and purchase criteria involved in the purchase decision and determine what role each of these criteria plays in the actual decision process.
- Determine what various types of information and information sources business customers use to select a product and to evaluate PPCI's products against those offered by the competition.
- Evaluate the extent to which customers consider/purchase services (i.e., warranties, etc.) at the time they make their desktop or laptop computer purchase.
- Identify the channels used by business customers when they purchase desktop and laptop computers.

293

Methodology

A Web survey was conducted among businesses in the US, UK and Australia. Respondents were screened to ensure interviews with qualified decision-makers who have purchased a qualifying desktop or laptop computer during the last six months. Respondents were considered qualified if they either make the decision or if they provide significant input into the purchase of specific desktop or laptop computers with this purchase decision/input including the brand decision for these products.

Additional quotas were set within each category:

- 60% desktop purchasers/40% laptop purchasers
- At least one-third of respondents must be PPCI customers.

Total interviews completed across the three countries were 1,500.

Five hundred interviews were completed per country, with 100 in each country being drawn from the following businesses size categories:

- Micro (1–10 employees)
- Small (11–100 employees)
- Medium (101–1,000 employees)
- Large (1,001–9,999 employees)
- Corporate/Enterprise (10,000+ employees)

PURCHASE PROCESS SUMMARY

As this is a follow-up to a prior survey, comparisons are made as applicable between waves of the study as well as between countries and company sizes.

- PPCI customers are price conscious and not as brand loyal as those who regularly purchase from major brand competitors. Only in Australia has there been an increase in business purchasers advising that they automatically look to buy PPCI products when needs arise and this is typically among the small to medium-sized businesses.
- Previous experience within a company is the main reason for initial brand preference across all company sizes and countries.
- Brand preference is, however, *more* of a factor in the purchase deci-

sion among micro and smaller businesses who are less likely to be linked in to a pre-approved brand list.

- The purchase process is the shortest among micro and small businesses where the immediate need for a product is typically more urgent than in larger businesses. The corporate/enterprise process typically takes an average of 2 weeks given the related requisition and purchasing documentation processes involved.
- Smaller firms are also more likely to purchase warranties on desktop and laptop computers and this is generally done immediately at the time of purchase. There has, however, been an increase in the US of medium-sized firms also seeking warranties and service programs at the time of purchase.

RESOURCES USED IN PURCHASE DECISION

- The Web is the key resource used by business purchasers when making a desktop or laptop computer purchase decision. While manufacturers' sites are relied on heavily, decision-makers frequently visit non-OEM sites to read product reviews and look at product comparisons.
- While advertising in press and periodicals does provide decision-makers with brand awareness, it does not typically sway their decision as it does not provide enough product detail.
- PPCI's Web site was rated much higher in this wave of the study, particularly in the US. It was noted that it has been revamped to be much more user-friendly and the purchasing capabilities have been simplified for those that wish to order directly versus through other channels.
- In the micro and small businesses, there is greater use of product brochures and point of purchase materials as these purchasers are much more likely to go directly to a retailer to make their purchase than are larger firms who may be placing multiple orders at one time.

CHANNELS FOR PURCHASING

- Two-thirds of medium-sized businesses purchase their desktop and laptop computers directly from the manufacturer, typically from the manufacturer's Web site.

- This figure is much higher in large businesses and the corporate/enterprise sector, where 83% are purchasing directly from the OEMs. This percentage has actually increased even since the initial wave of this study one year ago.
- Micro and small businesses are more likely to go directly to the retail stores to make their equipment purchases, although the percentage doing so in the UK is notably lower than in the US and Australia.

Appendix 5
Tales from the Trenches

Anecdotes from
International Researchers

Every researcher has at least one amusing story about a mishap or unusual circumstance that he or she has encountered during their career. It also probably goes without saying that these events are usually much more amusing when retold many months later than they are at the time they occur!

Several of my colleagues from both the vendor and client sides of the research process have provided examples of the types of entanglements you could possibly encounter during an international research project. The purpose of providing these anecdotes is not to scare you away from global research, but rather simply to show you how even the best-managed projects can hit unexpected "speed bumps" that somehow need to be handled, sometimes by unorthodox solutions.

Here are some situations that tested the researcher's resolve.

"Road to Singapore"

One marketing team was working on a packaging study conducted with a research supplier in Singapore. Singapore is a lovely, and for the most part, modern city, but technological advances were sadly lacking at this particular research facility. Rather than videotaping the focus groups, they videotaped *without* sound and then provided audiotapes obtained simply from setting an old tape recorder mid-table in the focus group room.

Storage was at a premium in this small building, so after the first evening of groups the project manager at the facility offered to lock the concept packages in one of the offices. The next day, when the client team returned for "round two," they discovered the only key to that particular office had gone home with a manager who was at that moment en route elsewhere in the country on a train. The project manager had to crawl through a vent and remove ceiling tiles, all the while trying desperately to avoid getting himself tangled in a myriad of wires and cables, and drop down into the office to get the necessary materials for the evening's focus groups.

While the project was completed on schedule, the client marketing team learned to expect the unexpected. ("Cat burglar skills" was added to the list of needed skills for future projects.)

"The Last Time I Saw Paris"

One project director recounts an experience in planning focus groups in Paris, which illustrates how the simplest plans can become tangled in the communications (or lack thereof)!

"In the days before purpose-built viewing facilities were available in every major city, it was common to rent two adjoining meeting rooms in a hotel and have the clients watch over a video link. This, and my lack of French, got me into hot water once when I was trying to book rooms in a Paris hotel.

"Having established from the switchboard operator that this hotel just cleared out bedrooms to use as meeting rooms, I proceeded to ask the conference organizer for 'two bedrooms, but they must be next door to each other, because I wanted to set up a camera in one of them so I can film what's going on and watch it from the other one.' After a very long pause at the other end, I made my excuses and rang off, too embarrassed to explain anymore."

"The Interpreter"

As mentioned in Chapter 3, in many focus group facilities abroad, the interpreter will utilize a sound-proofed booth from which his or her interpreted version of the groups is broadcast directly into the clients' viewing room either over a speaker or through headsets provided for each individual viewing the groups.

On one particularly stressful evening of focus groups, two of the primary research supplier's project managers took refuge in the interpreter's booth to escape momentarily from an extremely overbearing and rather "high-maintenance" client who was traveling with them. While the booth itself is sound-proofed, they did not realize that the interpreter's microphone had been left on during the previous focus group session and that their frustrations were being aired in their full glory to their clients and colleagues in the viewing room!

"Lost in Translation"

Traveling in any foreign country can be confusing, particularly when you are trying to get from one location to another in a hurry to meet your project schedule. For Westerners, this confusion is often magnified in Asian countries where few of the cabdrivers and local shopkeepers speak English, which makes asking for directions nearly impossible. One project manager discovered just how difficult this can be on a project trip to Tokyo.

"I left the hotel quite early for the focus group facility as I needed to arrive and brief the moderator and interpreter prior to the start of the evening's groups. I had obtained a translation of the address I was going to from the hotel concierge and was whisked away in a taxi in no time at all. The driver seemed to know where he was going at first, but then it became agonizingly apparent that he was lost, despite my effort to give him a translation from the concierge before we had set out. He made numerous cell phone calls and finally reached someone at the research facility who managed to guide him to the location. The entire trip took over an hour and a half and when we arrived, the facility was directly across the multilane street from my hotel!

"The research supplier's manager explained this phenomenon to me. While streets do have names in Tokyo, there are not many street signs. Directions are, therefore, given more often in terms of what landmarks (i.e., a certain bank or train station, etc.) the building is near versus relying on a written street address. Needless to say, the next evening I walked to the facility to attend my focus groups!"

"Out of Africa"

Researchers through experience have come to expect to encounter unusual circumstances over the course of international projects. Seldom, however, would one expect conducting a research project to be potentially dangerous.

Many years ago, a project director was conducting a research study about tourism development strategy. He shared his experience of ". . . a minibus full of . . . elderly American female tourists in a Tanzanian national park being repeatedly butted by a rhino until it fell over onto its side." This certainly gives a whole new perspective to putting your research project "in the field"!

"A Passage to India" (almost)

When you solicit proposals from suppliers in your home country for a domestic research study, you generally know what to expect in terms of their staff, quality and facilities. One research director, however, related a surprising experience with a prospective research partner in India. When one of the project managers visited the prospective supplier's physical site, he discovered that it was actually a soap factory trying to diversify its business a bit by conducting interviews as a sideline! This serves as one more warning about getting as many details as possible about your suppliers.

"The Road to Hong Kong"

While researchers have learned to adjust to different levels of quality in both focus group facilities and client service when taking a global project country to country, there is always room for the occasional surprise. One colleague tells of just such an experience she encountered during the development of a proposal.

"When asking an agency to quote for focus groups in Hong Kong, I received a bid which included 'van' methodology. This involves conducting the groups in a the back of a lorry parked in a central location to avoid costly facility fees. Apparently this is quite a popular way of conducting research in some parts of Asia, but not what my US clients, used to plush facilities, would have expected!"

"Once Upon a Time in Mexico"

It doesn't matter where you take your research on the road because if you are not on your home turf, there are bound to be unexpected complications as this situation clearly, albeit humorously, illustrates. One project manager had just completed a very detailed briefing in Mexico City for a client's research study to be conducted in numerous Latin American countries.

The study basically consisted of local interviewers intercepting customers who were in the process of shopping in the electronics departments of various major department stores. Customers were qualified for the study based on their stated intentions to purchase certain technology products in addition to meeting requirements through various other screening questions. The qualified customers then agreed to be "shadowed" throughout their shopping experiences. Interviewers were instructed to note in detail what these customers looked at, what they asked the sales representatives questions about and what, if anything, they ultimately bought.

The interviewer briefing had specifically stated that *once the customer left the electronics department*, the "shop" or interview was to be considered to be completed. This was true whether the customer actually left the store or whether he/she continued shopping in a different department. The first interviews went quite well and as planned, but in one instance, the interviewer appeared to have badly misunderstood the interview "termination" instructions.

The male interviewer followed the female customer as she left the electronics area and entered the lingerie department to shop for items of a slightly more intimate nature. The interviewer meanwhile dutifully continued to make notes on the questionnaire regarding what the customer was looking at and purchasing! This example provides still further evidence of the importance of clarity in both interpretation and detail in an international research project briefing!

"Once Upon a Time in Mexico" (Take Two)

Still another project executive offers an example of how miscommunications between you, the client, and your international research supplier can have somewhat dire effects on your research project. Once again, a study in Mexico was destined for confusion.

The client's focus groups were to be scheduled for a specific evening. The moderator arrived at the Mexican research facility only to find that, for reasons to this day undetermined, not a single one of the expected ten focus group participants had shown up for the group!

Apparently, the focus group facility coordinator had misunderstood the instructions and recruited participants for a different evening. Yes, of course, this could occur in your own domestic market, but the chances of such problems are increased when you take your research project abroad.

ENDNOTES

CHAPTER 2

[1] Depending on the type of research and the corporate sponsor, it sometimes can increase participation rates if the client is named at the beginning of the study because it allows respondents to feel they are helping the company.

CHAPTER 4

[1] See also the list of international research associations in Appendix 3.

[2] Note that this is a condensed version of the explanation of the methodology for the sake of the example. Formal proposals would generally provide a much more detailed explanation.

[3] Here the supplier would typically insert a table which breaks out the total research sample into quota groups for the proposed project.

[4] Estimated cost figures are deliberately not included as they may vary significantly by vendor, international exchange rates, etc.

[5] Given the fictional nature of this proposal, this section will consist only of bullet points regarding

what would generally be included in this part of the proposal.

CHAPTER 5

[1] "Global Online Populations," 2004, from the *Central Intelligence Agency's World Factbook, www.cia.gov/cia/ publications/factbook.*
http://www.clickz.com/stats/sectors/geographics/print. php/5911_15151.

CHAPTER 6

[1] Source: *http://www.executiveplanet.com/business-culture-in/132248561351.html.*

[2] Examples are drawn from *Dun & Bradstreet's Guide to Doing Business Around the World;* Morrison, Teresa C., Conaway, Wayne A., Douress, Joseph J.; Englewood Cliffs, NJ: Prentice Hall, Inc.. 1977.

[3] "Mind Your Manners," *Inc. Magazine,* September 2005, Roberts, Allen P., Jr.

[4] Source: *http://www.executiveplanet.com/business-culture-in/142018667328.html.*

CHAPTER 11

[1] Note that this is a fictional example. The reader should not rely on any suggested sampling, regional selections or "findings" presented in this "report."

CHAPTER 12

[1] Based on the ICC/ESOMAR International Code of Marketing and Social Research Practice (2001).

APPENDIX 1

[1] Source: *http://en.wikipedia.org/wiki*

INDEX

About TEXERE

Texere, a progressive and authoritative voice in business publishing, brings to the global business community the expertise and insights of leading thinkers. Our books educate, enlighten, and entertain, and provide an intersection where our authors and our readers share cutting-edge ideas, practices, and innovative solutions. Texere seeks to cultivate, enhance, and disseminate information that illuminates the global business landscape.

www.thomson.com/learning/texcre

About the Typeface

This book was set in Garth Graphic font. Based on a design by John Matt from the 1960's, Garth Graphic was reworked by Renee LeWinter and Constance Blanchard and released by the Compugraphic Corporation in 1979. A fairly strong old style face suitable for text setting; the heavier weights and condensed forms are most used for display work. The font was named after Bill Garth, a founder of Compugraphic.

Library of Congress Cataloging-in-Publication Data

Edmunds, Holly.
   The AMA guide to the globe : how to manage international marketing research / Holly B. Edmunds.
       p. cm.
   Includes bibliographical references and index.
   ISBN 0-324-31331-4 (acid-free paper)
   1. Marketing research. 2. Research—Management.
I. American Marketing Association. II. Title. III. Title:
American Management Association guide to the globe.
HF5415.2.E35 2006
658.8'3—dc22

                                                    2006011675

DATE DUE
